ASTROPUPS

LUCILLE CALLARD

Astrology Consultant: Jacqueline Chapple
Illustrations and Design: Peter E. Solomon

ASTROPUPS

Copyright © 2008 by Lucille Callard

ISBN:1-4392-17890
EAN: 9781439217894

Acknowledgements

We acknowledge, with gratitude, all of the helpful information and insights into various breeds from owners, trainers, breeders, and veterinarians. We couldn't have written this book without you.

Many thanks to Nicole Hill, EdM and to Loraine Volz, MSW for their editing skills and constant support, and to Lisa Eller for her hard work and dedication to the project.

General sun sign material applies to owning a dog and is not intended as a complete characterization.

It is noted that authorities world-wide differ on breed origins and evaluations. Various factors prohibit any guarantees by the author or the illustrator that any pup from any litter will develop as presented in the breed text or illustration.

AstroPups

Dedication

This book is for all of our beloved friends, past and present, steadfast and loyal:

Peggy, Bo-Bo, Pal, Roxie, Lucy, Hector, Apollo,
Sidney, Pua, Spike, Sam, Black Jack, Cocoa, Trixie,
Wrigley, Fenway, Tika, Samantha and Auggie

TABLE OF CONTENTS

A portion of the sale of each copy of *AstroPups*
will be donated to No-Kill Animal Shelters

INTRODUCTION

Our local vet remarked, ruefully, that he wished there was a way to match owners' personalities with dogs' temperaments. It took five years of extensive research and exploration, but we found a way to grant our vet's wish. We combined the ancient science of astrology with the established science of breeding to achieve compatible matches. In other words, we matched people's sun sign personalities with dogs' breed traits and temperaments.

We examined the twelve sun signs in depth to fully understand what kind of owner and trainer people born under each sign would be. Jacqueline Chapple, a professional astrologer and dog lover, helped us to understand sun signs' personalities. The next step was to research all of the purebreds registered with The American Kennel Club. Although the author is a canine behaviorist, who has studied and trained dogs for over twenty years, selecting the right purebreds for each sign was a challenge. In our research, we interviewed several owners of the different breeds, and found their information very helpful. Breeders and veterinarians gave us their experienced insights. We watched the dogs perform at numerous shows, and interviewed many trainers. Once the research was complete, we undertook the tremendous task of matching the sun sign personalities with the purebreds' traits and temperaments.

Astrology dates back to hundreds of years B.C., and was first explored by astrologers in the Middle East. Throughout the centuries it has been studied and developed by brilliant philosophers, scholars, and mathematicians. Kings and queens, classic writers, doctors, psychologists, and politicians have all made astrology a part of their work, and of their lives. Today, astrology continues to fascinate millions of people from all walks of life. This ancient science has a very modern application. It's proving to be extremely helpful in the current emphasis on relationships. Astrology helps people to understand themselves, and to understand others. Through *AstroPups*, astrology offers you insights on the kind of dog owner you are, and suggests purebreds compatible with your personality.

Deliberate breeding techniques have been used for centuries with dogs. Ever since dogs warmed themselves by cavemen's fires, they have served mankind. To meet the ever-growing demands man asked of his best friend, traits in certain dogs were studied and developed by selected breeding. Through trial and error, spanning many, many years, breeders were able to produce dogs that excelled in performing specific tasks. Some breeds trained well to the hunt, others could be relied upon to be aggressively protective, good recruits for the police, armed forces and customs. Some breeds were developed to be happy in the city, and others were bred for country terrains. Toy breeds became very popular as traveling companions. To keep breeds pure, official standard clubs were formed all over the world.

Because the study of astrology shows us that all living things are influenced at birth by where the sun was at the time, you may wonder why we have not matched people's sun signs with dogs' sun signs in *AstroPups*. Through our research, people have remarked that their dogs have quirks in their temperaments due to their birth dates, but it is a fact that purebred dogs, with good bloodlines, remain true to their breed traits and temperaments.

With this understanding, what if a dog, bred to be a town or city dog, such as a Boston Terrier, was born an Aries or a Sagittarius? Both signs are adventurous, but if you took this dog hunting, it would not only have difficulty finding your game, it wouldn't be able to find its way back to you. In all probability it would sit at your feet, shivering, dreaming of taking a nap in its own little bed. It's not a hunting dog.

Choosing the right dog is not easy! There are hundreds of breeds to choose from. They come in all colors, shapes and sizes with distinct breed traits and temperaments. When you decide to buy a pup, it's important to know all about the breed. Most puppies are cute, but you want the pup you choose to grow up to be a dog that fits in with your personality and lifestyle. All good relationships depend upon compatibility. *AstroPups* is a guide to help you to pick a pup that will grow up to be just the kind of dog you have always wanted.

Several purebreds have been selected to be compatible with your sun sign personality. Each breed is discussed in full to enable you to be an informed puppy shopper. Peter Solomon, a professional artist who has won platinum and gold awards for his creative artwork, has drawn the dogs selected for you. To find your perfect pup, check out the breeds suggested for you in your own sun sign chapter.

If someone else will be training and caring for your pup, the breed should be chosen from that person's sun sign chapter. People's sun sign personalities, and dogs' breed traits and temperaments have been carefully researched to make these matches. If the dog you choose is going to be a friend to the whole family, the primary caretaker's sun sign chapter is the one to explore.

As some of you know, astrology is much more than the general sun signs. Each individual has several contributing energies that make up his or her unique character and personality. For example, the moon's position at the time of your birth affects your emotions, and your Ascendant, also known as your Rising Sign, influences your outward personality. However, the position of the sun at the time of your birth is very significant. This is why astrologers in newspapers, popular magazines and on the Internet use sun signs for your day-to-day, or week-by-week general trends, and why we use them for your general personality.

If you are not sure of your sun sign because you were born on the *first* or *last* day of a sun sign dates, you should check with an astrologer to confirm what sign you really are. Sometimes the sun can, and does, move out of one sign and into the next sign on the same day. All you need is the date, time and place of your birth to verify your true sun sign.

Choosing a pup is exciting. When you pick the right one, a special relationship will begin from the first day you spend together. You will have made the choice, but the pup will be convinced it's the other way around, and claim you as its best friend for life.

Good Luck and Happy Hunting!

ARIES THE RAM
March 21 through April 20

Iron is your metal
Your stone is a diamond
Geranium is your flower
And your color is red
Now it's time to pick your purebred

"What's wrong with that dog?" some of you would definitely ask if you saw a Whippet peering out at you from under a chair. When you hear it's hiding because its owner lost her temper earlier, you'd soon lose interest. This dog is not likely to be your kind of dog, Aries. But before we start to name the breeds that we think would interest you, it's important to us that you understand where we're coming from.

Initially, as a professional astrologer and a canine behaviorist, our first question was, "What kind of dog owner would an Aries be?". We found the answer by thoroughly studying your sun sign personality. Once we knew what you would probably look for in a dog, we considered all of the breeds registered with the American Kennel Club to find some perfect pups for you. Now, we're not saying that you can only successfully own the dogs we have selected for you. What we are saying is that the pups we suggest would be good choices for you.

We'll first review the characteristics of your sun sign, and discuss dog traits and temperaments that would be a plus or a minus for you. Your compatible pups are then described in full so that you can make your own decision based upon your lifestyle and personal preference.

Your sign shows you to be a person filled with enthusiasm, and optimism. You are impulsive and bold. You were born under the first sign of the zodiac to be a leader and an achiever. When you have a goal, you focus on it, take risks, and go for it. You often win because you refuse to accept defeat. Some of you do this more quietly than others, but most of you are determined to succeed.

When something you've set your heart on is truly lost, you'll reluctantly throw in the towel. It won't be long, though, before you'll be off and running with a brand new goal.

You rarely ask for anyone's input. You're confident that your way is the right way, and the only way to go. You want others to be interested in what you are doing, but do not seek their approval The way most of you see it is, talking over your plans, and discussing options delays production. Taking action is your way to do things, and you'll take short cuts as the most direct route to success.

You're not always grabbing the world by its tail and trying to spin it on your own, though. In your vulnerable, quieter moments you seek companionship. You're affectionate to those you care for – a generous, loving person. However, you expect your love to be returned in full measure.

Most of you have a short fuse. You usually explode like a firework - scatter sparks, and burn out quickly. You can't understand why people want to go on about something that's over and done with. Wrongs and misunderstandings are much like failures to you, and you would prefer to forget them. If others wrong you, though, they could be forgotten along with the problems they've caused you.

To be the best is important to many of you. You are highly competitive. Winning is the only way to finish any game. You're not likely to plan the win with strategy and time-consuming game plays, though. Your direct approach affects everything you do. You lose some, of course, but this does not change your approach. Why spend time going over the whys of failures? You're too busy going for the next win.

Your personality is much like the spring – fresh and full of life. Your direction is forward, and you race along life's paths with youthful energy, even when your youth is long gone. Some of you are fearless, and go where few would tread, but that's because you believe in yourself and in your ideas.

Your strong, direct approach to all things will apply when it comes to choosing and raising a dog. If it's your own idea to get a pup, you'll be an outstanding owner for some breeds. Of course, there are some breeds that will respond to your no-nonsense approach and firm hand by hiding under the bed, and refusing to come out for a week. Your initial irritation will soon pass, but you'll probably forget the dog is under the bed.

Most of you will only respect a dog if it's both spirited and resilient. You don't like defeat in any form, and couldn't stand to see it in your dog's eyes or cringing behavior.

Intelligence is important in any breed of dog you own. Your dog must be able to learn what you want it to do. Many breeds are intelligent, but some of them are also very independent, and could choose not to obey you. That wouldn't do for you at all, Aries. When you give a command, your dog had better be listening, and obey that command.

An intelligent, but aloof breed can be trained to obey, but many of you would have a problem with an aloof dog. You'd need to spend a great deal of time working with, and winning this one, and most of you won't take the time to form the necessary attachment. You will expect your dog to want to please you, and to look to you for direction. It should also be a breed capable of great loyalty and devotion.

In fact, Aries, most of you would be reluctant to give room and board to a dog that falls short of your expectations in resilience, intelligence, obedience, affection and loyalty. You certainly wouldn't be proud of it, and that's important to you. You want a dog that others would envy – an outstanding breed.

Of course, there are breeds that have all of the above, but they move ponderously through life. These laidback canines would drive most of you crazy. Your dog should be able to keep up with you with an alert eagerness and enthusiastic nature to match your own.

Excessive grooming, and choosing the right ribbons for your dog's hair is not likely to be a priority for most of you. You might do this initially, but you are not likely to keep it up. Dogs who need constant grooming and decoration are therefore not suggested for your sun sign personality. Most of you won't mind brushing the dog, but it's doubtful you'll want to do more than that.

You'll expect a lot from your adorable pup, and you'll probably begin its training too early. It'll be hard for some of you to sit back and wait until the pup is old enough to do what you have in mind. Still, when your pup makes mistakes due to its youth or misunderstandings, you'll forgive and forget. You believe in yourself, and in your decisions, and you'll believe in the dog you've chosen. When your pup does learn the lesson of the day, you'll be so enthusiastic in your praise, it'll tumble over itself with joy, and probably perform again without being asked just to please you.

Finally, where you live, and your general lifestyle are important considerations when picking a pup.

The first dog suggested for your sun sign personality, Aries, is definitely ready to be a part of a winning team, and could be just what some of you are looking for.

GERMAN SHEPHERD

Colors: Black, black and tan, gray
Height: 22" – 26"
Weight: 77 – 95 lbs.

If you choose a true German Shepherd pup, you'll be the owner of a breed hailed as a champion all over the world. A Shepherd is spirited, resilient, intelligent, and learns with an alert eagerness.

Shepherds are very trainable by good handlers, which is why the police, military, and customs recruit them. They are also in great demand as guide dogs for the blind as they are capable of being very loyal, and are usually devoted to their owners. In addition to their utilitarian value, they are also superb show dogs, and have taken home the champion's cup on both sides of the Atlantic.

Firm, direct, positive training is the way to go with this pup, but you'll have to find the time for serious training. It's a dominant breed, and needs your leadership and direction. Left to its own devices, with only intermittent training, the dog could decide for itself who and what to dominate. Of course, it's not likely that you'll allow this to happen. It's a rare Aries who takes orders from a family member. Besides, when you have an achiever like a Shepherd, it's both challenging and exciting to train the pup to its full potential.

As its name suggests, the breed is German, and was first brought to the U.S. post World War I by soldiers returning home. Since then, the dog has become extremely popular. When quantity and not quality is sought, bloodlines suffer. Many of you are impulsive. *Don't buy the first pup you find unless you have checked on both the breeder and the pup's background.* You deserve the best, and with a little extra effort, you can find a real purebred.

German Shepherds shed. You'll need to brush the dog regularly. Brushing your dog will not appeal to some of you, but there are two important reasons why you should do this yourself. Brushing your Shepherd will strengthen the growing bond between you, and believe it or not, the action of brushing and stroking your dog can lower your blood pressure. Although most of you rarely give more than a passing thought to such things, you'll be helping both you and the dog to stay healthy.

When your pup is about three months old, it's important to *socialize* it with as many friendly adults, children, and dogs as you can in pleasant circumstances. Twelve weeks is the dog's special imprint time. Socialization will not affect the dog's natural guarding instincts, but it will help the dog to be more at ease with strangers for the rest of its life.

As a guard dog, show dog, and companion, a true German Shepherd is hard to beat, but if you're looking for a more sporting, all-purpose breed, this one is special.

WEIMARANER
Color: Gray
Height: 23"-27"
Weight: 70 – 85 lbs.

The spirited, graceful Weimaraner has a nickname among sportsmen.

They call it the *Gray Ghost*. In the fields during dusk, light reflects off its metallic coat, and its pale eyes shine. There's nothing ghostly about its performance, though. It's a superb gun dog and bird retriever.

There are several things that many of you will particularly like about this dog, Aries. Weimaraners train to the hunt much earlier than most hunting dogs, and they excel at tracking. If you're wondering how brave they are in unknown terrain, German hunters once used this breed to track down wild boar, and hold them at bay. The police recruit them for their intelligence and trainability, and they do well at show, especially in Obedience Trials. As companions, they are both protective and loyal.

Your strong personality and direct no-nonsense style of training is good for this breed, but if you want the best from your pup, *you'll have to count to ten when handling it*. Most Weimaraners are sensitive to their owner's moods and feelings. Lighten up when training, and use a positive approach. If you lose your cool too often, the pup will become confused. There'll be no confusion when it catches on and performs well, though. Your enthusiastic response will mean more to the pup than its reward treat.

Because Weimaraners have fine, soft coats, housing them outside in winter in most states is not possible. When on a hunt, though, weather is not a concern. The dog keeps warm by working hard. You won't have to spend much time grooming this one. Weimaraners do not shed, and keeping your pup clean is easy. In fact, some Weimaraners groom themselves, just like cats.

Although it's a fairly large breed, it adapts to apartment living well, so long as you give it enough exercise.

President Eisenhower's dog, Heidi, increased the breed's popularity. There was some indiscriminate breeding to meet the public's demand at that time but it's now fairly easy to get a real purebred.

Weimaraners have the reputation of being good all-purpose dogs. The dog will strive to please you, Aries, when mutual trust has been achieved. The breed has enough spirit, intelligence, speed and style for even the most demanding among you. However, if you are a serious duck hunter, and intend to hunt where the water forms ice crusts, here's the breed hailed as "the best".

CHESAPEAKE BAY RETRIEVER
Color: Brown or tan
Height: 21" – 26"
Weight: 65 – 80 lbs.

The Chesapeake Bay Retriever is a powerful, muscular dog. The breed was named after Chesapeake Bay. The story goes that a ship went aground there, and two pups were given to the rescuers. These two pups were the originators of the breed.

You will admire the strength of the Chessie, Aries, and you will be impressed by its courage, determination, and tenacity. However, this dog is bred for one purpose only – hunting water game.

Your strong, firm handling is needed for a Chesapeake, and early control is advisable. *Your pup must be trained in the basics before you introduce it to water.* If your Chessie hasn't learned to obey your commands, it won't want to come out of the water even for a liver treat.

An *untrained* Chessie will probably leap into any body of water, particularly if there are ducks about. If you live by the ocean, and your untrained Chessie is missing, it's not likely that you'll find your dog on the beach. You might be able to spot it, though, swimming towards the horizon chasing the gulls.

Most of you love a good challenge, and your Chessie will give you one. No hunter would ever want to change the Chesapeake's cultivated traits and temperament even if that were possible, but anyone who owns a Chessie admits it's a hardhead. This dog is as enthusiastic about its pursuits as most of you are, and it never gives up on its quarry. That's something most of you would appreciate, Aries.

Your way is a good way for this one, but it's important to connect strongly with your pup. All your hunting dog needs is to be confident about where its loyalty lies, and then it will give you its best, not only on a hunt, but also as a protective and good companion.

Unlike the Weimaraner, apartment living is not for the Chessie, nor is house living. This breed is best kenneled outdoors. Its double coat and hard-working oil glands enables it to swim in freezing water, but it has a strong doggy odor in confined spaces.

German Shepherds, Weimaraners, and Chesapeake Bay Retrievers are all protective dogs, but here's a breed bred to guard, and is favored by many guard dog trainers.

ROTTWEILER
Color: Black and tan
Height: 22"- 27"
Weight: 95 – 135 lbs.

Rottweilers have had some bad press, and deservedly so. It's more than probable that indiscriminate breeding, mismatched owners, and poor training were the causes for the dogs' behavior. A Rottweiler is not a dog that anyone should pick casually for a pet, even though the dog is capable of great loyalty and affection. As a pup, this dog is totally adorable - a chubby, cute, squirming puppy, but it will grow up to be a large, solid, muscular dog with an aggressive temperament. *It's obsessive about guarding its family, your possessions, and its territory.*

The breed was named after the town of Rotttweil in Germany. It was once known as the butcher dog because its primary function was to drive cattle to slaughter. Nowadays, the police, armed forces, and customs recruit Rotts. The breed is highly intelligent, and with the right training, excels.

One of the main problems many of you will have with this breed, Aries, is the time the dog takes to mature. As is usual with many of the larger breeds, your Rottweiler will stay a pup for a very long time – a large pup! In fact, *you will not have a mature, trained dog for about two years.* There are no short cuts with this project, but if some of you can handle the wait, a Rott is well worth waiting for.

Lighten up initially, and control with pup with a light hand. As the pup grows, your firm, direct approach will be just right. One thing you won't have to do is to teach the dog to guard. It will do this instinctively. You will have to direct the dog as to what you want it to guard, and from whom. It's not a good idea to let your dog make those decisions on its own. Your strong personality and leadership qualities will set your dog right when it tries for dominance, and it will soon learn that you are Alpha – the leader of its pack.

It's important to *socialize* your pup when it's three months old, the special imprint time for all breeds. Take the pup out to meet and greet friendly people and other dogs for the next month or so. This is especially important if you intend to make your Rottweiler your companion. Socialization of your pup will not affect its guarding abilities. What it will do is to help to stabilize the dog's temperament at social occasions or in crowds. It will also help the dog to distinguish between friend and foe for all of its life.

City apartments are not the best homes for this one. The dog is muscular and needs a lot of exercise. In addition, a small area to guard tends to make the dog overly protective.

If you don't push your Rottweiler pup too early, and train it with firmness and affection, you'll own an outstanding, obedient, loyal guard dog.

For those of you looking for an attractive, furry dog, our next suggestion is a magnificent Spitz breed.

ALASKAN MALAMUTE
Colors: Shades of gray, sable, black or red, always with white.
Height: 23" – 25"
Weight: 75 – 85 lbs.

The Alaskan Malamute is from the Spitz group, and has been traced back to possibly 3,000 years, bred by the Mahlemuits tribe of Alaska. It has a long work history with man, and miners who came to Alaska during the gold rush of 1896 used the dogs to haul their rock debris away in wooden carts. Malamutes helped Admiral Richard Byrd to the South Pole, and Jack London and Rudyard Kipling focused upon the Malamute in their wonderful stories.

The breed has a similar disposition to you, Aries. It loves to be part of the action, is high-spirited, and can be bold on occasion. It can also be quite dignified, observing the world through calm, proud, almond-shaped eyes.

The dog eats to meet its needs, its appetite varying according to how much exercise the dog gets. It's a strong and muscular dog that needs to run and play daily. For this reason, city apartments are not the best homes for Malamutes. They are quiet and well behaved in the home, but penning them up in small spaces really puts a strain on their robust natures.

If you live where it snows, your Malamute will be in its true element. If cart trained, you can hitch the dog to a sled, and your dog will thoroughly enjoy pulling you and the kids through the snow.

The Malamute is a family dog, but this does not necessarily extend to other family pets. Some authorities believe that the Malamute was once bred with wolves, but whatever the reason, some Malamutes are not good with small animals, or at times with other dogs. *Socialize* your pup at its special imprint time of three months with as many dogs and people as you can in pleasant circumstances. This will help the dog and you, too!

Your dog will rarely bark, so it's not considered a watchdog. If you hear a wolf howling in the back yard, it's your Malamute. They also talk – sounding like Chewbacca in the *Star Wars* movies. Chewbacca's sounds were based upon a Malamute named Indiana, once owned by George Lucas.

You'll find Malamutes in hot climate states, but in truth, hot climates are hard on them. Their outer coats are thick and coarse, and under coats dense, oily, and wooly. They shed their heavier coats in the summer, but there is no way to avoid the brushing your Malamute will need year round. Don't forget to give its tail a brush, too. It curls over its back like a question mark.

This breed is intuitive. If the dog senses that its owner is the indulgent type, it will surely take advantage. As a pup, it's absolutely adorable, and some find it hard to discipline this furry charmer, but discipline is just what it needs. Firmness is the way to go. You'll expect the dog to learn and to obey, and luckily for your Malamute, you usually give second chances. It will accept your leadership, but it's not naturally obedient. You have leadership qualities, and your Malamute can learn. Certainly Malamutes have done really well in Obedience, and star in the show ring.

When you walk your Malamute, be prepared for the fuss people will make when they see your dog. Few can walk passed this one without stopping to admire and appreciate how handsome this dog is.

German Shepherds, Weimaraners, Chesapeake Bay Retrievers, Rottweilers, and Malamutes are all large dogs with definite traits. If your lifestyle prohibits you from owning a large breed, and your tastes run to a smaller model, there are smaller breeds that have enough courage, spirit, intelligence and loyalty for dogs ten times their size. This next breed is one of them.

FOX TERRIER – SMOOTH AND WIRE
Color: White with black or tan markings
Height: 14"-17"
Weight: 20 - 25 lbs.

A Fox Terrier is as highly spirited, and as adventurous as many of you are, Aries. It's a very intelligent breed, able to learn a number of things, but you won't have to teach it to protect you and yours. This is one of the Fox Terrier's reasons for living.

Originating in England, this terrier was named for its ability to bolt foxes from wherever they were hiding, and in the past ran with the hounds. In addition to being very agile, it has great endurance. A happy Fox Terrier has boundless energy, and is eager to participate in whatever you or your family may be doing. A family Smooth, named Peggy, even loved to join in a sing-a-long. Great crooner, even if she was a bit off-key.

There's little grooming, and the pup can handle hot summers outdoors. The Smooth is very popular in India because ticks and fleas find it hard to burrow into its short, fine coat, and the dog handles India's climate well.

If you get a Wire, grooming is important, but some of you will find the effort rewarding because a well-groomed Wire Fox Terrier is a beautiful dog.

Foxies love the show ring. They exhibit themselves with pride, have a spirited stance, and an upright tail. Your enthusiastic, competitive nature will delight your pup – it wants to win as much as you do.

If you choose a Fox Terrier, you'll have a lively pup on your hands. It's as feisty as they come, full of mischief, and will need your firm hand from the start. Don't come on too strong, though. This dog's jaunty spirit is what makes it special enough to win Best in Show all over the world. If you are too strict when it's a pup, you could damage what makes it so very special. Initially this pup sees life as one big game, and gets quite creative in inventing variations. Let your sense of humor win, and go along once in a while. It's a great way to bond with a Foxie. Fortunately, this breed genuinely wants to make you happy, and will literally jump through hoops to do just that.

One thing you can't do, Aries, is to ignore the dog. If you do, it will get into trouble very quickly. Bored, lonely and at odds, the dog will amuse itself by getting into a lot of mischief. Most of you do not live alone, though, and this terrier enjoys the whole family.

Socialize the pup at its imprint time of twelve weeks. Introduce the pup to all the nice people you can find. It has a friendly nature naturally, but can be highly strung. This pup will love meeting all the strangers you can muster, and thoroughly enjoy the experience of being admired by all.

Fox Terriers are extremely popular dogs. You would be wise to check out the breeder and bloodlines of the pup before you buy one. When quantity and not quality is sought, bloodlines usually suffer.

There is a miniature of this breed known as **TOY FOX TERRIER.** Similar to its bigger cousins, the Smooth and the Wire, it's a delightful little dog. The toy breed is very popular in Australia where it's commonly known as the Mini Foxy.

Terriers are lots of fun. Here's a little one especially suited to apartment living.

CAIRN TERRIER
Color: Red, gray, salt and pepper
Height: Up to 12"
Weight: 13 – 16 lbs.

The Cairn is an old Scottish breed, skilled at chasing foxes that hide among the ancient burial stone piles called Cairns. The dog became famous when Cairns were cast as Toto in *The Wizard of Oz.*

Aries, you're sure to like the spirit wrapped up in this small package. A Cairn wouldn't hesitate to challenge a German Shepherd if one dared to set foot in its yard. It's a very loyal and good little watchdog.

Like most terriers, a Cairn is nosy! Your pup will take an interest in whatever you may be doing. When it gets underfoot, though, a sharp word will send it scampering to its bed. It will watch for a change in your mood, and as soon as you laugh about something, the dog will be back at your side. Cairns are very quick to learn what you expect from them, and equally as quick to learn what they can get away with. Your firm and positive way of training will bring the dog to obedience quite quickly, particularly if you have a dog treat handy when the pup does well. The pup will enjoy learning all kinds of tricks, but you won't have to teach it to sit up and beg. The Cairn does this very nicely all by itself.

Cairns love showing off to the judges. They trot around the ring confident and proud of themselves. If you intend to show your dog, you'll need to have the dog professionally groomed. If your dog is not heading for the show ring, it has a coat that needs trimming and brushing. Tangles make a Cairn uncomfortable, and it could lose its sweet disposition if you don't take care of that.

Your Cairn will enjoy a walk, and will love to ride in any car you drive. If you leave the dog at home, alone, though, it will keep itself busy watching over the place in your absence, and playing with its toys. You'll get an enthusiastic welcome when you walk back through the door.

The German Shepherd, Weimaraner, Chesapeake Bay Retriever, Rottweiler, Alaskan Malamute, Fox Terriers, and the Cairn are the breeds we have selected to be compatible with your sun sign personality, Aries. We hope we have been of help to you.

Good luck in picking your perfect pup.

German Shepherd

Weimaraner

Chesapeake Bay Retriever

Rottweiler

Alaskan Malamute

Fox Terrier

Cairn Terrier

TAURUS THE BULL
April 21 through May 21

Copper is your metal
Your stone is a sapphire
A rose is your flower
Pale pink is your color
And you favor pale blue
Now let's find the right pup for you

If a neighbor's dog bounded into your yard, Taurus, most of you would probably grin. You like dogs. However, if the dog refused to obey its owner's command to return home, the dog would cease to amuse you. An independent, disobedient breed is just not your kind of dog. Before we start to name the breeds that would interest you, though, it's important to us that you understand where we're coming from.

Initially, as a professional astrologer and a canine behaviorist, our first question was, "What kind of dog owner would a Taurus be?". We found the answer by thoroughly studying your sun sign personality. Once we knew what you would probably look for in a dog, we considered all of the breeds registered with the American Kennel Club to find some perfect pups for you. Now, we're not saying that you can only successfully own the dogs we have selected for you. What we are saying is that the pups we suggest would be good choices for you.

We'll first review the characteristics of your sun sign, and discuss dog traits and temperaments that could be a plus or a minus for you. Your compatible pups are then described in full so that you can make your own decision based upon your lifestyle and personal preference.

Your sign shows you to be a person who is full of determination. On the surface most of you appear to be easy-going, but you can be as firm and as stubborn as necessary to protect your rights, especially in your home. You'll be fairly indulgent with the youngest members in your family, but you'll rarely back down on issues of importance to you, even for them.

Most of you are not impulsive. You'll make your decisions after careful deliberation. Once you have reached a conclusion, it's almost impossible for anyone to change your mind.

You are deeply rooted in the traditional, tried-and-true way of doing things. Spur of the moment schemes hold little interest for most of you. They are not practical. Most of you are stable, and this is why people tend to rely upon you.

Kindness is part of your personality, Taurus. You can be particularly gentle with those you love. You are protective of your family members, and are loyal to them. Many of you are good parents, spouses, or lovers because you take your commitments seriously.

However, it is not always easy for you to show your feelings. Most of you tend to keep your problems to yourself or within the family group. Outsiders do not often win your trust because you are as cautious with your emotions as you are with everything else. Love is not the only feeling you move into slowly. Anger is another. It's usually hard to get you riled up about anything. Although your patience is quite remarkable, you can be pushed too far, and if this happens, you can erupt like Mount Vesuvius!

Fortunately you keep that incredible temper of yours under wraps throughout much of your life. You don't suffer fools gladly, but you won't let them get to you too often. On a day-to-day basis, most of you are conventional, down-to-earth people, full of common sense and practicality.

When it comes to kids and pups you're not likely to lose your temper. Sure, you might snort a little, even bellow when they go too far, but most of you are patient and indulgent with youngsters. Your pup will be treated in much the same way as you would treat a favored child. Most of you are particularly tolerant with a youngster who has won your heart. However, to stay a favorite, the child must learn to listen. Your pup must do the same. This is why it's important for you to choose the right pup, Taurus. It would be hard on you if the pup could not settle down, listen, and learn when you have made it a part of your family.

We'll now discuss traits and temperaments in breeds that would be a plus or a minus for your Taurus personality. An independent dog might give some of you a problem. It will be more interested in its own pursuits than in yours, and could refuse to come when you call. You may consider its self-interest to be disloyal, and loyalty is high on your list of requirements for any friend. It's embarrassing to be ignored by your dog, too. Although it's not personal on the dog's part, many of you will take it personally. A dog ready and willing to give you some respect in return for its room and board would be better for most of you – a loyal and devoted dog.

Now a loyal and devoted dog sounds good, but how should your dog behave in your home? Your home is very important to most of you. It's your place to relax - to get some peace. When you come home after a hard day at work, you want to kick back, put your feet up, watch TV, listen to music, or read. Where should your dog be? Snoozing close by in a companionable way, of course. What you don't need is a wired dog leaping about, sending anything not nailed down flying, ever ready to leap on you and to slurp your face with doggy kisses. If you choose a very active, highly-strung breed, you might hope it will settle down. Actually this dog will probably twitch in its sleep. It's probably a dog that needs a five mile run daily, and for most of you, that's not likely to be on your daily schedule. Give your kind heart a break, and get a dog that likes to stretch out quietly in a comfortable spot as much as you do.

A loyal, devoted dog that shares quiet times with you sounds more like it, right, Taurus? But what if your home is suddenly filled with noisy people? Many of you love to entertain and you do it very well. Your dog should be a part of your party, but should not be annoying to your guests. It should be a breed that does not insist on joining you at the dinner table. A dog that is friendly, but not intrusive, would be appreciated by most of you.

Docile in the home is one thing, but most of you will want to see some spirit and bounce in your dog when you take it for a walk. Some of you love to stroll through the woods – to feel as one with nature. If you live in the country, you'll often relax this way. If you live in the suburbs, you'll know where the forest preserves are, and if the city is your home, you'll find the most beautiful park. Sharing your walks with your dog will appeal to most of you, and if the dog is an eager participant, it will add to your own enjoyment.

Most of you will probably want a conventional type of dog at the other end of that leash, though. Fad or fancy breeds won't impress many of you.

To sum up, Taurus, your dog should be loyal, devoted, well mannered in the home, and spirited outdoors. And, because you have a sensual nature, which gives you a sensitive touch, you would enjoy petting a dog with a soft or silky coat.

You'll be an excellent owner for some breeds. When your dog has the traits and temperament to suit you, you'll become very attached. You'll laugh with the pup when you play together, and, as the pup grows, and trains well, you'll be responsive and affectionate. Most of you will form a close bond with your canine companion, and be rewarded with its devotion for all of its life.

When you consider the dogs we have suggested for your personality, Taurus, consider your lifestyle also.

The first breed we have selected for you is known as "the armchair clown". Some of you will love this one.

BASSET HOUND

Colors: Black/white/tan, red/white, pale tan/white
Height: 14" – 15"
Weight: 40 – 80 lbs.

Few people will understand the Basset as well as you, Taurus, and give this pup the kind, firm handling it needs. In the home it's slow moving and easy-going. Taking a nap is one of its favorite things to do. If you rustle the treat box, though, or open the refrigerator door, the dog is by your side in a flash. One of the first things this pup learns is the sound of snacks, and how to beg effectively. Since you also seek the good things in life, this may amuse you, but you'll have to be firm to be kind. A fat Basset is not a wholesome sight. It waddles about on its short legs, trying to keep its tummy off the floor.

Fortunately, there's another interest for a Basset – going for a walk. On the scent in the country is a Basset's favorite outing, but exploring the local woods in the suburbs is fine, too. If you live in the city you'll need to locate a wooded park or your Basset could lose its feisty outdoor spirit. Tracking on concrete just doesn't do it for this hound.

When you put on your coat, and reach for the dog's leash, your Basset will quiver with excitement. Once outside, its at-home personality disappears. Your Basset becomes a hunting dog and is incredibly agile for its stature. It was the French who bred this dog to be a badger hound, and if there's a badger within a five-mile radius, your Basset will let you know with its hound sound!

This breed's tracking skills can be observed at the Basset Hound Field trials, which is something you may want to look into if you are interested in training your pup for competition. For those of you interested in showing your dog you'll find the Basset to be a proud contestant. In the show ring, Bassets trot with dignity.

Your patience and tolerance is needed to raise and train this pup. You'll probably be indulgent when it's small, for a Basset pup is a charmer with a constant comical expression. At first, it can't find its center of balance. Its body is too big for its legs, and the pup falls over itself as it scampers across the floor. You'll need a baby gate if you have stairs. Without one, the pup is sure to take more than a daily tumble, which could do serious damage, and prevent its healthy growth.

Much like the larger breeds, a Basset grows out of its puppy stages slowly. If you push a Basset too hard, and too soon, the dog could become stubborn. It's not a breed given to quick obedience and tends to mull over its options like most of you do. Dog treats work the best when training this pup, but the way you handle the dog will win it over more than anything else. A Basset is delighted to find an owner who is easy-going and understanding about its puppy efforts. Once the dog has learned to trust and love you, Taurus, it becomes devoted. Obedience will follow.

When your Basset has formed an attachment to you, it will lie in your spot whenever you are not around. This is probably on the most comfortable armchair in the home. Not only is it a warm cozy place to take a nap, it smells like you. Now that's Heaven to a snoozing Basset. If you are occupying the chair it will settle down at your feet. When you reach down to pet the dog, you will do so with pleasure. A Basset's coat is short, soft and silky.

Hush Puppies, as Basset Hounds are sometimes called from the shoe ads, are certainly lovable, but if you are strong physically and looking for a watchdog of size and substance, check out this one.

SAINT BERNARD

Colors: Orange, deep red brindle, red-brindle with white
Height: 25" - 34"
Weight: 120 – 180 lbs.

Owning a Saint is a true commitment. It's not a dog anyone should choose lightly, but that's not a problem for most of you because you usually weigh all of your decisions carefully. In your deliberations consider the cost of feeding a Saint.

Although a Saint Bernard is an enormous dog, a pup bred from good lines is as gentle as it is powerful. This breed is known for its devotion, faithfulness, and protectiveness. To win a Saint, you should train the dog without aggression. Its puppy stages move slowly. If handled with kindness and patience, the pup will grow up to be exceptional.

There are smooth and rough Saint Bernards. The rough is more popular for show. Its coat is beautiful, longer and curlier than the smooth, and feels silky on its massive head. You'll need to groom both types, but some of you will enjoy this task, sensing the bonding this promotes between you and the dog. You'll also enjoy how handsome your dog looks when groomed well. It's a good idea to start getting your Saint used to grooming when it's a young pup.

Your Saint pup is big to start with, but it has no knowledge of size. It will make repeated attempts to be a lap dog. The pup will not feel hurt if you wisely reject its efforts, and get on the floor to give it a hug.

This breed is intelligent, and will train well. One of the things you will not need to train the dog to do, though, is to guard you. This it will do instinctively. Saint Bernards are well known for protecting the monks at hospices in the Swiss Alps. Not only do they protect their masters, they also serve as guides over the mountain passes. The breed became famous when the dogs helped to rescue lost mountain climbers and injured skiers. Rescuing and protecting is in a Saint's blood. In the U.S., several dogs have won medals of valor for rescuing children trapped in burning buildings or in danger of drowning.

Saints love children. Unfortunately, their size is a problem in this respect as they knock down toddlers in their enthusiasm to show their affection. Once a Saint is trained, though, a child can safely play with the dog like a giant soft toy. The dog is tolerant with most children.

Now although your dog will instantly adopt children, Taurus, this does not apply for adult strangers. Your protection is always on your dog's mind, and it will treat strangers in your home with quiet suspicion. It's a good idea to *socialize* your pup at about three months old by introducing it to as many friendly adults as possible in pleasant circumstances. Twelve weeks is the special imprint time for all pups, and will help your pup to be more comfortable with strangers in your home for all of its life. Your dog's instinctive guarding abilities will not be affected by its socialization.

If it is necessary for you to chain or cage your dog, Taurus, don't get a Saint. It's important for this breed, when trained, to be allowed to roam its own territory freely. When caged, or chained for long periods, the dog is no longer placid. The breed is descended from the giants used in the Roman Arenas, and those dogs were undoubtedly caged until Showtime. This does not prohibit your using the crate method for puppy safety and care, providing you get a big enough crate. However, the adult trained Saint Bernard should not be on the end of a restrictive chain or locked up in a small area.

Saints are super dogs, but if you are a more sedentary Taurus, looking for a dog that needs little exercise or grooming, the mascot of the U.S. Marines may interest some of you.

BULLDOG
Colors: Black, black and white, black and tan, brindle
Height: 12" – 14"
Weight: 40 – 60 lbs.

There are few breeds that can match the Bulldog for devotion, Taurus. This is a very loyal dog. If the pup is raised the right way, it will grow up to be a dog that would give its life to protect you. In fact, the Bulldog's courage, tenacity, and devotion are legendary. It's not surprising that the marines chose this dog for their mascot, Yale University adopted it, and the British made it their national dog.

Long ago, the Bulldog was used to bait bulls. It's an intelligent breed, learns very well, if not quickly, and once trained, it never forgets the rules. However, this dog is quite a character. The British are responsible for the Bulldog, and in our opinion, being British ourselves, it's possible that the dog has adopted some of their ways to avoid an argument. If the dog doesn't want to do what you have asked it to do, it prefers not to make a fuss. Instead, it might suddenly appear to have gone deaf, start to limp painfully, or even lie comatose. Before you call your vet, call your dog, rattle its treat box, or open the 'fridge door. It's amazing how all of its symptoms disappear if there's a chance of a tasty tidbit.

Bulldogs, like Basset Hounds, love good food as much as most of you do. If you share too often though, you'll regret it. An overweight Bulldog is hard to live with. It wheezes, snores, and could offend your Taurus nose with gassy explosions. The dog will retain its powerful, muscular figure, and its dignity, if you keep its snacks down and take the dog for short walks. Don't plan on jogging with this one. It will try to keep up with you, and before long, it'll be wheezing, huffing, and puffing. Regular around the block walks are all that's necessary.

There's little grooming needed, but many Bulldogs enjoy the attention of being brushed. To increase the bonding between you and the dog, groom once or twice a week. You, Taurus, should be the one who feeds the dog. Bulldogs take a note of these things, and care for those who care for them.

Basset Hounds are good companions, and St. Bernards and Bulldogs good protectors, but perhaps you are looking for a sporting, all-purpose breed.

LABRADOR RETRIEVER
Colors: Black, chocolate, yellow
Height: 21" - 24"
Weight: 55 – 80 lbs.

It's not surprising that Labs are one of the most popular dogs in the U.S. It's truly an exceptional dog. As a pup it will strive to please you, Taurus, and you will soon become very attached. Highly intelligent, easily trained, and capable of great devotion, a Labrador Retriever would definitely qualify as your best friend.

The breed originally came from Newfoundland, was refined in Labrador, and enthusiastically adopted by the British. It's an excellent hunting dog, good in the field and in water. Labs are literally tireless, and ignore bad weather conditions. If you intend to hunt, you'll find this dog very responsive to learning the rules. The dog's obvious love of the sport and the outdoors makes it an ideal hunter's companion.

If you don't hunt, your dog will love to run in the woods, and will find it hard to ignore its natural instincts. Hector, a black Lab in our family, brought us live pheasants or ducks. He carried them to us in his soft mouth. The birds were complaining but unharmed.

It's a good idea to keep a few of the dog's toys close to the front door, Taurus. On your arrival home, your dog needs to give you a present and will seize anything close to hand. Tika, a Chocolate Lab we know and love, always grabs a shoe, and if your Lab chooses to do the same, it's hard to match up a pair on a busy morning. This trait comes from when the dogs were praised for retrieving downed quarry by their hunting owners. It's impossible to untrain this trait, Taurus, and if you try you'll have a very confused pup.

There is a difference in the colors of the breed in our opinion. Black Labs are mellower. Yellow labs are beautiful, but need firmer handling, and Chocolate Labs are usually more highly strung. You would be a good owner for all the colors of this breed, Taurus, because of your patience and understanding of the pup's sincere efforts to work with you. The bond will grow quickly between you, and your pup will scamper after you wherever you go. This pup has a need to attach, and it will develop well with an affectionate and companionable owner.

Labs get along with children very well, and usually like most adults. However, they can be quite choosy about visiting dogs. Your firmness, along with your affection is necessary to keep the dog under your control. *Socialize* the pup at its special imprint time of twelve weeks with as many friendly people and canines as you can find. It will help the dog to be more relaxed in crowds and in strange surroundings.

It's not a good idea to leave your Labrador alone for long periods. If a Lab is denied human companionship it can become quite depressed. If things don't improve, your lovable canine friend becomes mournful. This is not likely to happen with you, though, Taurus. Most of you usually take care of your own.

The next breed is also a sporting dog, which we think some of you will really relate to.

CLUMBER SPANIEL
Colors: White with lemon or orange markings.
Height: 17"- 19"
Weight: 70 – 85 lbs

It's possible that the French crossed the now extinct Alpine Spaniel with a Basset Hound to achieve this breed. After the French Revolution, Clumbers were bred mainly in England, and were a favorite of King George V.

The Clumber Spaniel is known for its great heart, patience, and perseverance. It seeks peace in its home, but loves to walk through the woods and fields. As a hunting dog, the Clumber is slower than other spaniel breeds, but is dependable and reliable. It's a good dog for rough shooting.

To develop the pup's full potential, it's important to understand the breed. Aggressive behavior and harsh demands will actually impede this dog's ability to learn. Because most of you are patient and kind you'll allow the pup to grow at its own steady pace, and it will grow up to be a serious, dignified dog that performs well on command.

You'll need to groom a Clumber, and it might be wise to check with your vet about avoiding possible ear problems. Grooming such a steady, reliable dog is a pleasure, and will help to cement the bonding process.

As show dogs, Clumbers do well, and have won Best in Show at major events.

If you have children, and they do not abuse the dog, your Clumber will become their friend. Clumber Spaniels strive to please. When you give your pup your approval, your dog will wag its whole body, but then, it doesn't have much of a tail to wag.

Spaniels do well with most of you. Here's another that might interest some of you.

COCKER SPANIEL
Colors: Black, black and tan, fawn, buff, cream, black and white, red and white.
Height: 14" - 15"
Weight: 23 – 28 lbs.

Spaniels are an old breed, and possibly date back to Egyptian times. Drawings of dogs resembling spaniels were found in tomb excavations. Their name, however, does suggest Spanish origins. Why this particular spaniel is called a Cocker is because the dog once excelled in hunting woodcock. Hunting rabbits is also one of their favorite things to do. They are a hardy breed, and have lots of stamina.

Although some hunters have used Cockers for a close hunt, and have spoken well of them, this breed is now much more popular as a pet or for show. A show Cocker is outstanding, but needs constant grooming of its profuse coat. Professional attention is required about four times a year. If your dog is not headed for stardom, though, you can keep its coat short, and this will cut down the grooming work considerably. It's important to get the tangles out of its silky hair as they are painful and take the pleasure out of being petted.

Most Cocker Spaniels adore their owners. They have a very affectionate nature. It's very important to be indulgent with a Cocker pup, though. It will try hard to please you, and if its efforts are off the mark, due to its youth, scolding the pup would be a mistake. Punishment could cause the pup to become timid, especially at its imprint time of three months. Patience and kindness, along with firmness, is a must when training this pup.

This breed has been popular for a very long time, and quantity over quality is the result. It's important to know what to look for when choosing your puppy. A scared, timid pup might appeal to your protective instincts and kind personality, but you should not adopt it. The friendly, outgoing pup will need you just as much if it is to develop to its full potential. Besides, a timid pup, growing up to be a fearful dog would probably irritate you when there's no apparent reason for its behavior.

If a Cocker is allowed to develop in a pleasant atmosphere, this pup is a mischievous, merry youngster. It loves to play and romp outside. Going for long walks is one of its favorite things to do. In the home the dog is well behaved, and will stretch out happily beside you. Cocker Spaniels are not large dogs, and can live wherever you do.

Our next suggestion is favored by British royalty and is a good breed for apartment and suburban living.

PEMBROKE WELSH CORGI
Colors: Red, sable, fawn, black and tan with or without white.
Height: 10" – 12"
Weight: 25 – 30 lbs.

Beloved by the British royal family, the Pembroke Welsh Corgi has been a part of their family for decades. Queen Elizabeth owns several of them.

The breed's name comes from the Celt word for dog. Corgis came to Wales in the 12th century with Flemish weavers, and the Welsh used the dogs for herding cattle. The little dogs nipped the heels of straying animals to keep them in line.

A Corgi would rather play than fight, and usually adores children. Nevertheless, it's still a watchdog, and is protective of its territory. Strangers will be treated with suspicion. *Socialize* your pup at its special imprint time of twelve weeks. Introduce it to as many strangers and other dogs as possible in pleasant circumstances. This will help the dog to be more relaxed when strangers come to your home.

You would be a good owner for this one, Taurus, because at times the dog gets over excited, stimulated by hyperactive people. Your matter-of-fact handling of the dog, and your kind heart will keep the dog on a steady course. You won't have to persevere with its training though. Corgis learn their lessons earlier than most breeds, and if you want to show it as a young dog, it will behave well in the ring.

You'll need to brush and comb your dog a couple of times a week to keep its coat in good condition.

The Pembroke has an inquisitive nature, and loves to explore its neighborhood, town or country. Walks are important for this sturdy, hardy little dog.

Like most of you, it loves good food and will beg tidbits. It's hard not to give in to its charming manner of begging. The Pembroke has such an appealing little face, and very expressive eyes. Being overweight is a serious problem for all dogs, but more so for dogs with short legs. Since you are practical, and take care of your own, most of you will watch the dog's diet to keep the dog healthy – well most of the time anyway.

It would be difficult not to fall for a Pembroke once it becomes a part of your family. It's a charming little dog with one aim in life – to please you.

The Pembroke has a cousin who is also a sweetheart – the **CARDIGAN WELSH CORGI**. It has a bushier tail, and bigger ears. Although similar in appearance it is classified as a separate breed. The Celts brought the dog from Europe to Cardiganshire in Wales in the 12th century. Like the Pembroke, the dog was used on farms to herd cattle.

In temperament the breed is less outgoing than its cousin, and is a quieter dog - less perky, but still ready for a game with a ball. If you want to show your dog the Cardigan is very easy to prepare for the ring, and usually behaves well when traveling. It's a good breed for apartment living, but loves to go for a walk. There'll be no scrappy dogfights with this one as Cardigans behave with decorum.

The Pembroke is more popular on both sides of the Atlantic, but the Australians favor the Cardigan. Check them both out. Either one will win your heart.

If, however, you are looking for a Toy, we suggest a breed you will understand very well.

KING CHARLES SPANIEL
Colors: Black and White
Height: Up to 10"
Weight: 10 – 15 lbs.

This aristocratic little spaniel has been a member of court for centuries. Van Dyck painted several portraits of King Charles with his spaniels in the 17th century. The dog was known as the Toy Spaniel, but it became the King Charles due to its favor with the king.

Variations of the King Charles Spaniel are the **PRINCE CHARLES** (white with black and tan markings), the **RUBY** (chestnut red) and the **BLENHEIM** (white with red markings). A larger breed was developed in England from the Toy Spaniels and is known as the **CAVALIER KING CHARLES**. This spaniel can weigh up to 18 lbs., and is usually the color of the Ruby or the Blenheim.

The King Charles Spaniel is not temperamental. It's a very steady, level-headed little dog, full of affection for its owner once a bond has formed. It doesn't like to be rushed into new experiences, and likes to take its time. At first you will find your pup shy, but once it gains confidence, and gets used to the home and family, it fits in nicely. If you own a cat, the King Charles will probably seek it out for a best friend.

The dog enjoys the outdoors. It's a hardy breed, but if the dog gets wet it's important to towel it dry, and to make sure its bed is dry and clean. You should bathe its face after an outing outdoors. The little dog is inquisitive, and could get dust and grass particles in its eyes.

Check with your vet about ear care.

Grooming is an easy chore for the dog's coat just needs to be brushed weekly with little or no trimming required. Exercise is needed daily to keep the dog fit. It loves its food, and will turn its liquid eyes on anyone in the family that's eating something that smells good. Indulgent owners cause the dog to become obese.

Sweet, affectionate and playful, Toy Spaniels are very special and it's not surprising that they roamed palaces for centuries, beloved by kings, and have now become very popular pets, adored in countless homes.

The next breed suggested for you, Taurus, is a Toy terrier breed, popular in the U.S.

YORKSHIRE TERRIER
Color: Steel blue with tan markings
Height: 8" – 9"
Weight: 4 – 7 lbs.

Yorkshire Terriers are amongst the sturdiest of the Toy breeds. Sky and Black and Tan Terriers with a touch of Maltese are believed to be in the breed recipe for this one, originating in West Riding, Yorkshire, England.

Yorkies are wonderful pets with good watchdog traits. They are fiercely loyal and extremely protective. Bright, and easy to train, this breed has done quite well in Obedience trials. In fact, the dog's intelligence, along with its courage was noted by the military, and Yorkshire Terriers were once war dogs. They were trained to carry communication lines through narrow pipes.

As hunters, they made excellent ratters, and will go to ground for rabbits. The Yorkshire Terrier is a very versatile breed.

As feisty as they come, this pup will need your firmness, along with your tolerance, to teach the dog that you are the boss. Totally unaware of its size, your Yorkie will try to dominate you. If the pup decides it has won this first round, it will then decide who is allowed to enter your home. It may be small, but it can be quite fierce. Of course, it's not likely that most of you will allow such goings on.

To teach the pup that you do not necessarily need protection from all strangers, *socialize* it at about three months by introducing it to as many friendly people as possible in pleasant circumstances. You'll have to make sure that the pup is handled carefully, though. Three months is the pup's special imprint time, and a bad experience will defeat your purpose.

If you plan on showing your dog, the grooming is extensive. A Yorkie's coat is very long, fine and silky. If you don't plan on showing the dog, though, keep its coat trimmed, and brush regularly. Shedding is not a problem, but tangles are. Grooming your pup will help the dog to know who is Alpha – the leader of its pack – and will help the bonding grow between you.

If not coddled, and handled to retain its spirit, a Yorkshire Terrier is a lively, affectionate companion, always listening for the sound of your voice.

The Basset Hound, Saint Bernard, Bulldog, Labrador Retriever, Clumber Spaniel, Cocker Spaniel, Pembroke and Cardigan Welsh Corgis, King Charles Spaniels, and Yorkshire Terrier are the breeds we suggest for your sun sign personality, Taurus. We hope we have been of help to you.

Good luck in picking your perfect pup.

Saint Bernard

Basset Hound

Bulldog

Labrador Retriever

Clumber Spaniel

Cocker Spaniel

Cardigan Welsh Corgi

Pembroke Welsh Corgi

King Charles Spaniel

Yorkshire Terrier

GEMINI THE TWINS
May 22 through June 21

Mercury is your metal
Your stone is agate
Lily-of-the-Valley is your flower
Your color is orange - rainbows please you, too
Now lets find a pup that's as versatile as you

If you bought a sweet pup that grew up to be a dog that lay about like a log most of the time, you'd probably think it was a dud, Gemini. You're not likely to respond too warmly to permanent snoozers. Before we name the breeds with traits and temperaments that would interest you, though, it's important to us that you understand where we're coming from.

Initially, as a professional astrologer and a canine behaviorist, our first question was, "What kind of dog owner would a Gemini be?". We found the answer by thoroughly studying your sun sign personality. Once we knew what you would probably look for in a dog, we considered all of the breeds registered with the American Kennel Club to find some perfect pups for you. Now, we're not saying that you can only successfully own the dogs we have selected for you. What we are saying is that the pups we suggest would be good choices for you.

We'll first review the characteristics of your sun sign, and discuss dog traits and temperaments that could be a plus or a minus for you. Your compatible pups are then described in full so that you can make your own decision based upon your lifestyle and personal preference.

Your sign shows you to be a person with a very versatile personality. Your interests are broad, and you welcome the chance to check out something new or unusual. Most of you have masses of energy and people enjoy your participation.

For most of you, living a humdrum existence is downright depressing! You need variety and stimulation to keep your sparkle alive. If you're in a routine setting, where everything is predictable, you'll either play the clown to break the monotony, or play the blues. Restrictions stifle you. You need freedom to expand your horizons both at work and at play.

If your job is run-of-the-mill, too routine, the *Classifieds* will probably become your favorite section of the newspaper.

Investigating new fields is exciting, but if circumstances force you to stay in a job that holds little interest for you, you'll probably have hobbies that help to jazz up your life. Most of you hate sitting about doing nothing but passing the time. In fact, being actively involved in something stimulating is vital to your well being.

It's really important for you to be able to communicate. Some of you chat a lot, and if you are unable to do so face-to-face, there's always the telephone. Others prefer to communicate through the written word. You usually have lots to say. Your mind is quick and often creative. Even if you appear to be a quiet person, your thoughts run from sprints to marathons.

Most of you love to debate. Debating is something you have been doing ever since you learned how to think. You are, after all, Gemini the Twins, and often debate with yourself on several matters. Of course, you can offer significant arguments for both sides of most questions, and sometimes have a problem deciding on the best way to go. This can be confusing at times, but there's no switch in the world that can turn off your Gemini mind.

Some of you definitely look for such a switch at night when, just as you are about to drift off to sleep, something pops into your head, and you're off and running again. Resting, relaxing is difficult for many of you, which is why you often relax through active pastimes such as board games, puzzles, drawing, writing or surfing the internet.

Most of you are rarely loners. There are times when you need to be alone to sort out something that's bothering you, but most of you are quite social folk. Casual relationships often appeal to you, as they do not force you into unwanted commitments. In addition, the more people you know, the more chance there is of spending your time off in a variety of activities.

There are times when your world actually stops spinning for you, Gemini, and you need a good friend to hug. The right kind of dog could be just such a friend. It will cheer you up when you feel down, and help you through lonely times.

You'll probably train your pup with a light, affectionate hand, with occasional bursts of discipline when the pup goes too far. It's not likely that most of you will be a strict disciplinarian. You are too busy with your own lives. Many of you will thoroughly enjoy teaching the pup tricks, playing and romping with your dog.

Let's now take a look at the traits and temperaments that could be a minus or a plus for your personality, Gemini. They contribute greatly to the breed choices suggested for you.

In your need to share your life with someone, to communicate what's happening for you, most of you look for an active listener. When you come home alone, you'll probably confide in your canine buddy. If the dog lies there, like a log, and barely stirs itself to welcome you, you'll be quite put out. You'd certainly label the dog as totally boring.

Well some dogs are like that in the home, but it would be hard to convince you that it's not personal. No welcome except for a thump of its tired tail? You'll expect your dog to leap up to welcome you home, and then follow you about, eager for your company. That's the kind of dog you'll want to come home to.

An aloof breed may disappoint you in a similar way to one that is inactive in the home. Some of them will interest you because they are beautiful to look at, and appear to be mystical with that far-away look in their eyes, but if your dog lives in its own world, it's not going to be overly concerned with yours. The dog may quietly walk away in the middle of your story, or decline your offer to romp and play. Clearly it's not seeking your company. A dog that is always interested in what you are doing would be much more fun for you.

Now a pup from an aggressive, dominant breed will certainly be alert to what is going on in your life. It will follow you about the house, and even turn its head to one side to try to understand what you are saying. It will race after a ball you have thrown, and challenge you to play some more. You'll love its intelligence and quickness to respond to you, Gemini. Sounds like a perfect pup for you? The problem is that when the pup becomes an adult dog, it will require a strong boss. You may be an excellent boss on Wednesday and Thursday, but what about Friday and Saturday? You could become busy, and let up on its training and control. Consistent rules are not your Gemini style, but dominant breeds need them. It would not be long before your dog took advantage of your mind-elsewhere days, and make some inappropriate decisions on its own. In addition, Gemini, you prefer to avoid people who try to control you, so you certainly don't want to adopt a dog that challenges your authority daily. A pup from a breed that will appreciate your more casual style without taking advantage - a flexible dog - would suit you better.

Most of you will adore your pup, share its antics with all of your friends, and take it out and about with you to show it off. Of course, things will settle down, and other interests will come your way. The dog will then spend a fair amount of time on its own. Even though it misses you, it should be able to cope with your absences. You don't need to worry about a pining dog in your home, especially if it refuses to be cared for by anyone but you. When you leave for a long period an over-dependant dog could refuse food and water, and spend its time mournfully peering out of the closest window to the door, watching, waiting, and whimpering.

A dog that's pining for you because you are busy elsewhere would definitely touch your heart, but what if you got a pup that decided not to accept the situation with sad, doggy laments? This dog could be a breed with good problem-solving skills. Its problem is your absence. Its solution is to get out and find you. You could come home to a carpet tunnel, chewed doors and walls, and the custom-made living room drapes in a pile on the floor. Your home probably has some style and flair in its décor, but now it'll look as though a demolition crew stopped in while you were out.

Your life, Gemini, would be much easier if you chose a pup from a breed that will stay contentedly by itself, or a social dog that also loves other people, such as the neighbors, the teenager next door, a dog-sitter on first meeting, and most friends. Then, when you are away, you'll have one thing less to worry about, and the dog will be happier too.

To sum up, the right pup for you, Gemini, is one that is eager for your company, lively in and out of the home, playful and affectionate. It should not be a dominant breed. As an adult dog, it should be able to handle your absences without pining or being destructive. The dog should be friendly and outgoing. In addition, your pup should be from an intelligent breed, quick to train and easy to handle.

When you are checking out the pups suggested for your sun sign personality, consider your lifestyle at the same time. The first breed we think some of you will like comes in three sizes.

POODLES

Colors: Black, white, brown, cream, coffee, apricot, silver and gray
Height: **Standard** over 15" **Miniature** over 10" **Toy** 10" and under.
Weight: **Standard** 65 lbs Miniature 20 lbs **Toy** 14 lbs

Of the three sizes of this breed, we think the **Miniature** is probably the best size for your sun sign personality, Gemini. Standards are certainly impressive, but require consistent handling due to their size, and Toys although very sweet, tend to be over-protective and jealous.

Some of you will absolutely adore the Miniature Poodle. It's intelligent, quick thinking, alert, active, and very affectionate. It will watch over your home in your absence, and welcome you back with great excitement, eager to hear all about your day. Because it learns quickly, and wants to please, it's not hard to train. Many of you will enjoy this one as it loves to learn tricks, which it will enjoy performing when friends drop by.

Poodles are bred with two different types of coat: thick and woolly or long and corded. They shed little and are clean dogs, but both types of coat need trimming and grooming.

How they look affects how they feel. An untrimmed Poodle with a tangled coat is a sad sack. It loses its cheeky spirit, and positively droops! You'll probably relate to this, Gemini, as most of you have some flair and style in your own appearance.

The Germans originally bred them as a sporting breed. The German word *Pudel* means to splash. Trimming Poodles was originally done to help them to swim more swiftly when retrieving game. Later, when it was found that Poodles enjoyed learning tricks, and performed them with style, grooming them attractively became a part of their costumes in the circus ring. If you have a talent for grooming, a bath and a regular trim will suffice, but if you intend to show your dog, you'll need a professional who understands the strict requirements for a Poodle on center stage.

Although this breed loves to be a star in the circus ring, or taking the honors in the show ring, its main goal will be to star for you. As social as this pup is, *it chooses its favorite person quite early on, and remains loyal throughout its life*. It would be wise to be a constant for this pup at three months – its special imprint time. Take the pup out to meet other pups and people for a couple of weeks, during this time also.

Poodles' bloodlines have suffered because of its popularity, and in particular this applies to Miniatures and Toys. Quantity over quality was sought. Shop carefully for your pup before you buy one. Check on its background. Any reputable dealer will have this information on file.

Sophisticated, yet affectionate, Miniature Poodles would be a good breed for some of you, but perhaps you are looking for a solid breed that needs very little grooming.

BOXER
Colors: Fawn or brindle with white markings
Height: 21"- 25"
Weight: 55 –70 lbs

The Boxer we know today started in Munich, Germany in 1896. Opinions vary but it's thought to be descended from the Tibetan Mastiff, with some Bulldog and possibly Great Dane in its mix. The breed was first registered in America in 1904, and its climb to popularity was slow at first until people learned the dog had a very sweet nature, and Boxers took the honors at Show.

Although the Boxer is a large dog, it's happy in an apartment, town house, country mansion, cottage, or suburban home. When trained, it's extremely well behaved. You'll respond to its affectionate nature, and its keen interest in whatever you may be doing or saying. In fact, Boxers love to communicate as much as you do, Gemini, and are intuitively wise to their owner's moods.

Because these dogs are responsible in the home, intelligent, and easily trained, they have become favored guide dogs for the blind. They are also K-9 recruits for the police and army. Boxers are known for being able to serve in whatever capacity required of them. They have an even temperament along with an inquisitive nature, keen mind and social graces.

Although your Boxer enjoys hanging out with friendly people, when you leave it at home alone it will play happily for hours with its toys. Of course, you may find that old teddy bear you saved from childhood missing. Check your dog's bed. You'll probably find it stashed next to the green squeaky frog, rubber ball, one of your socks, and a rawhide strip.

If you have children, your Boxer will love them. Kids are wonderful playmates for a dog that, even when old and gray, always wants to play. *If you have cats, though, don't get a Boxer.* Some Boxers find a cat chase impossible to resist, delight in treeing felines, and will spend hours tracking them down in the home.

If you live where the winters are cold, you'll have to go shopping for sweaters for this one. Its coat is very fine and soft, and doesn't keep out the chill winds. Save your old towels, too. When your Boxer has been out in the rain, it will need you to dry it off. If you live where the summers are hot, air conditioning is a must. Boxers shiver in the cold and pant in the heat.

Is it a guard dog? Opinions differ on this question, and it's possible that the dog behaves according to whether it feels an intruder intends bodily harm. Samantha – *see front cover* – alerts her owner to a passerby with low growls and barks. She's definitely a good watchdog.

Most Boxers do not respond well to total strangers, and are wary of them. *Socialize* your Boxer pup by taking it out to meet and greet people, and other dogs, at its special imprint time of three months. It would also be a good idea, Gemini, if you did not get the pup when you plan to be away a lot. Just like the Miniature Poodle, your Boxer will choose its favorite person, so make sure you are a constant with your pup during its imprint time.

When people have had a Boxer as a member of the family, they rarely want any other breed. It's just that kind of dog. If, however, you are looking for a more sporting breed, you will appreciate the speed and the gentle nature of this one.

BRITTANY SPANIEL
Colors: White with red or orange patches
Height: 18" – 20"
Weight: 30 – 40 lbs.

You may come across this breed in black and white, and liver and white, but red or orange and white is usually favored with the dog's eyes dark amber, and its nose pinky-brown. Its coat is soft and silky with light feathering on its throat, stomach and legs. A Brittany Spaniel is a very attractive dog.

It's possible that France and Wales came up with the dog that we know today, as Welsh Springer Spaniels are similar to the Brittany. The breed was not registered with the American Kennel Club until 1934.

This dog is gentle, eager to please, and is highly intelligent. *If, however, the pup is punished harshly it will not grow into its potential.* Most of you wouldn't think of treating your puppy harshly, though, so the pup should be safe with you.

If you hunt, or are interested in Field Trials, you'll find that the Brittany has a dual personality. It's courageous and tough in the field, but gentle and devoted as a pet. Speed at the hunt is the Brittany's style. It's very quick, agile, and has no fear of brambles. At times, it does lose its concentration when affected by other stimuli, but we think that you'll understand this minor flaw, Gemini. If you give your dog a firm, but friendly reminder to stay on task, your Brittany will excel. The breed has done well at the American National Field trials.

The dog is sensitive, Gemini, so don't forget to introduce your Brittany pup to friends, strangers, and other dogs at its critical imprint time of twelve weeks. It'll help the dog to feel more comfortable at social gatherings for all of its life. Everyone will respond to this sweet, soft, wriggly bundle of charm. Introduce your pup to water in a fun and easy-going way, also, so you can have fun with your Brittany at the lake or at the ocean.

If you live in the country or in the suburbs, you'll have a happier spaniel. The dog loves to go for a walk, and to be able to use its excellent nose in the woods and trails. Be sure you have trained your pup before you unclip its leash, though. It could scent something fascinating and take off with incredible speed.

The dog's coat will need regular brushing and trimming from time to time. It would be wise if you could find the time to do this yourself, Gemini. You should start early, taking over where the pup's mother left off. Grooming your spaniel will cement the bonding process. Of course, most of you like to do two or more things at the same time, so as you groom you could play music, and sing softly to your pup. It'll love the sound of your voice, even if you sing off-key.

Spaniels often have ear problems, but you can check this out with your vet, who can advise you on the preventative medication to use.

The Brittany is a good sporting dog, but if you are looking for a smaller companion-watchdog, this one is a sweetheart.

WEST HIGHLAND WHITE TERRIER
Color: White
Height: 10"- 11"
Weight: 15 – 18 lbs.

This little dog will put a grin on your face most of the time, Gemini. The Westie is fun. Not only is it an outgoing little dog, it's bright, loves to play, is a good watchdog, and very affectionate.

Originally bred to flush badgers and foxes from hiding places in the rocky terrains of Scotland, the Westie came in all colors. However, multi-colored dogs were sometimes mistaken for the game they flushed. They were then bred to be all white for their own safety. The breed was once known by many other names, too, Pittenweems, Poltallochs, and Roseneaths - named for the areas in which they lived. In the early 1900's the name West Highland White became official.

The Westie made its debut in show business at *Crufts* in London, England in 1907. Nowadays it's a breed to contend with competitively. It seems to enjoy being on center stage at Show, and is a pert, happy participant, usually delighted to meet the judges.

Your Westie will quickly learn what you expect, and will be eager to please you. However, determination, along with an inquisitive nature is part of the Westie's charm. You'll have to be firm at times without being too harsh or punitive.

A regular brush and trim keeps this little dog looking smart. It has a double, thick coat that enables it to handle all weathers. Just like you, it loves to go out into the world. If you decide to take your dog along, most Westies travel well. When the dog stays home alone, it will take its job as watchdog quite seriously, and give you an enthusiastic welcome when you return. If you plan on being away for a long time, your Westie will probably get restless. Some Westie owners buy a pair if their lifestyles include long absences from home. If you are a part of a family, or live with friends, your Westie will miss you, but will be contented with them. It's a sociable little dog.

Our next suggestion for you is a dog that has the look of an aristocrat, but the sweetness of an affectionate child.

WELSH TERRIER
Colors: Black and tan, grizzle and tan
Height 15"
Weight: 20 lbs.

The Welsh Terrier resembles the King of Terriers, the Airedale, in looks, but is more predictable in traits and has a less aggressive temperament.

When you first see this pup, it will probably look all black at its true colors take about twelve weeks to come in fully – which is the dog's special imprint time also. As the colors emerge, you'll find this pup to be most attractive.

Write the date in ink on your calendar for the dog's socialization time, Gemini, as some Welshies can be shy with strangers if not *socialized.* Take your pup out to meet and greet as many dogs and friendly people as possible at twelve to fourteen weeks.

Descended from the black and tans, the Welsh became a separate breed over a hundred years ago in Wales. The dogs ran with the hounds on a foxhunt, and worked on the farms helping to round up livestock. Its first classification was at Caernarvon in the mid 1880's, and the breed arrived in the U.S. in 1888. The dog was shown at Westminster in the beginning of the 1900's and from then on, its popularity increased.

Most Welsh Terriers adore their owners and love to be a part of family and friends. Because it has a calmer nature than most terriers, it exhibits an impressive amount of self-control. It's an intelligent dog, Gemini, and will be eager to please you. Of course, it will also hope you'll be up for a game or two on a regular basis and one of its first presents should be a ball. Your pup will soon learn where you keep its leash also.

If you intend to show your Welsh, a professional groom is advised. Since most of you will want your dog to look its very best at all times, you'll probably do this anyway even if you don't intend to enter the dog in competition. Between visits, the dog will still need to be brushed regularly.

This dog will guard your home in your absence, and will be delighted when you walk back into its life. You'll warm to the Welsh, Gemini, because beneath its look of arrogance is a gentle and affectionate dog.

A look-a-like to the Welsh Terrier, and similar in many ways, is the Lakeland Terrier. It has a feisty, lively spirit, and is intelligent. You won't find it hard to train, and the dog usually exhibits good manners in the home. However, the pup will need a firm hand as it tends to get over-enthusiastic and makes some inappropriate choices when given free reign.

Once known as the Patterdale Terrier, this breed was bred and raised in the Cumberland lake district of England. Its primary job was to hunt down foxes that invaded the sheepfolds. On a scent, the Lakeland is relentless, refusing to give up on its quarry, and has been known to go underground for several days. Digging is one of their favorite things to do, which you might want to keep in mind if you have a landscaped garden.

Lakeland Terriers thoroughly enjoy strutting their stuff in Show, and have done very well. They were accepted for AKC registration in 1934. You'll need a professional to groom your dog for Show, but if you decide to avoid competition, you'll still need to hand strip its coat twice a year, or take your dog to a professional who will do it for you.

Although the Welsh and the Lakeland look alike, there are some differences in the two breeds for those who know them well. The Lakeland has a louder and more insistent bark than the Welsh, and tends to be more excitable, but both terriers are easily trained and are loyal and protective family members.

Don't forget to *socialize* your Lakeland pup at its special imprint time of twelve weeks. It will help the dog to accept visitors to your home more easily. As an adult dog, the Lakeland is very serious about its job of guarding you and your property.

Terriers are lots of fun. The next breed suggested for you, Gemini, is special in many ways.

SHETLAND SHEEPDOG (SHELTIE)
Colors: Tricolor, sable or white, blue
Height: 13"- 16"
Weight: 14 - 16 lbs.

Once a Sheltie has attached it becomes a part of its owner. The dog is so highly attuned to its owner's whereabouts, it actually senses when he or she is close to home, and is at the door long before the key turns in the lock.

The breed is Scottish. It's thought that the Border Collie is in its mix. The English Kennel Club recognized the breed in 1909, and the first Sheltie, Lord Scott, was registered with the AKC in 1914.

It's a three-purpose breed – an affectionate pet, fine show dog, and an alert watchdog. Actually, it's quite a good baby sitter, too. Shelties often follow their young charges about to herd them from harm.

A Sheltie will not accept your visitors easily. The dog is usually reserved with strangers. Since you probably entertain a lot, introduce your pup to friendly people and other canines at its special imprint time of about twelve weeks. *Socializing* the dog will help it to be less suspicious of friends dropping by, but will not affect its protective instincts. It takes its job as a watchdog very seriously.

Undue harshness would quickly destroy a Sheltie's trust. Aggressive and punitive treatment would drastically change this dog's natural sweet behavior. Your easy style of training, with expectations of good behavior is good for this breed. Intense training is not necessary. The dog is intelligent and extremely eager to please. Using a firm voice will quickly bring the dog to obedience.

A Sheltie will not invade your space, but it does like to keep you in its sight at all times. When it takes a nap, it is more contented if this could be inches from your feet.

Outside the dog is very lively, and likes to play. You'll find it behaves well on long walks. On your return, your Sheltie will probably clean up its paws

Brush your Sheltie's coat once a week to keep it looking smart, and if you intend to show your dog, a professional is advised. You might want to enter the dog in Obedience. It has done well here.

Hot climates are not very good for a Sheltie as the dog was bred to withstand the harsh winds and damp, cold weather of the Scottish moors. It's a good dog for the city, country or the suburbs, though.

Shelties are sweethearts, but perhaps some of you are looking for an aristocratic, stylish Toy. If so, you will find this one very appealing.

PAPILLON
Colors: White with patches of any color but liver
Height: 10" – 12"
Weight: 8-11 lbs.

It's pretty obvious why the French named this breed Papillon, which is French for butterfly. The dog has heavily-fringed ears which look like a butterfly in flight. A variation of the breed has drop ears, and is known as the Phalene, meaning moth. Both British and Belgian breeders developed the Papillon for recognition, and the dog was first shown in Britain in 1923. The U.S recognized it in 1935. However, the Papillon is an ancient breed and appears in paintings centuries old. The dog was highly favored by the French and Spanish nobility. It's said that Marie Antoinette cuddled her beloved Papillon for comfort as she walked to the scaffold.

Although this dainty little dog looks as though it needs pampering, a Papillon is both hardy and resilient. The dog loves the outdoors, and would enjoy a walk of several miles. If a walk is not on its schedule, it will play happily in the yard, chasing birds, butterflies and spiders. It's a friendly pup and because it's intelligent, it trains quickly and easily. You will not have to train it to protect you and yours, though. All intruders will be warned away with sharp barks.

Your pup's coat is silky and soft, and although it's not prone to matting, it can get tangles. You'll need to brush them out, and its fringes will need a trim. The Papillon's tail is somewhat like a spitz breed in that it curls over its back. On the Papillon it looks like a French plume. In parts of France, they call the butterfly dog the squirrel dog for this reason.

European nobility adored Papillons because these pretty dogs loved them back with total devotion and loyalty. The drawback to these admirable qualities in a Papillon for you Gemini is that the dog tends to become very possessive. *Socialize* the pup, with care due to its size, at its critical imprint time of twelve weeks. Meeting lots of friendly people at this time will help the dog to share you with your friends. Of course, it will still gaze at you with total adoration, but for some of you, that will be more than okay.

The Miniature Poodle, Boxer, Brittany Spaniel, West Highland White, Welsh and Lakeland Terriers, the Sheltie, and Papillon are the breeds we suggest for your sun sign personality, Gemini. We hope we have been of help to you.

Good luck in picking your perfect pup.

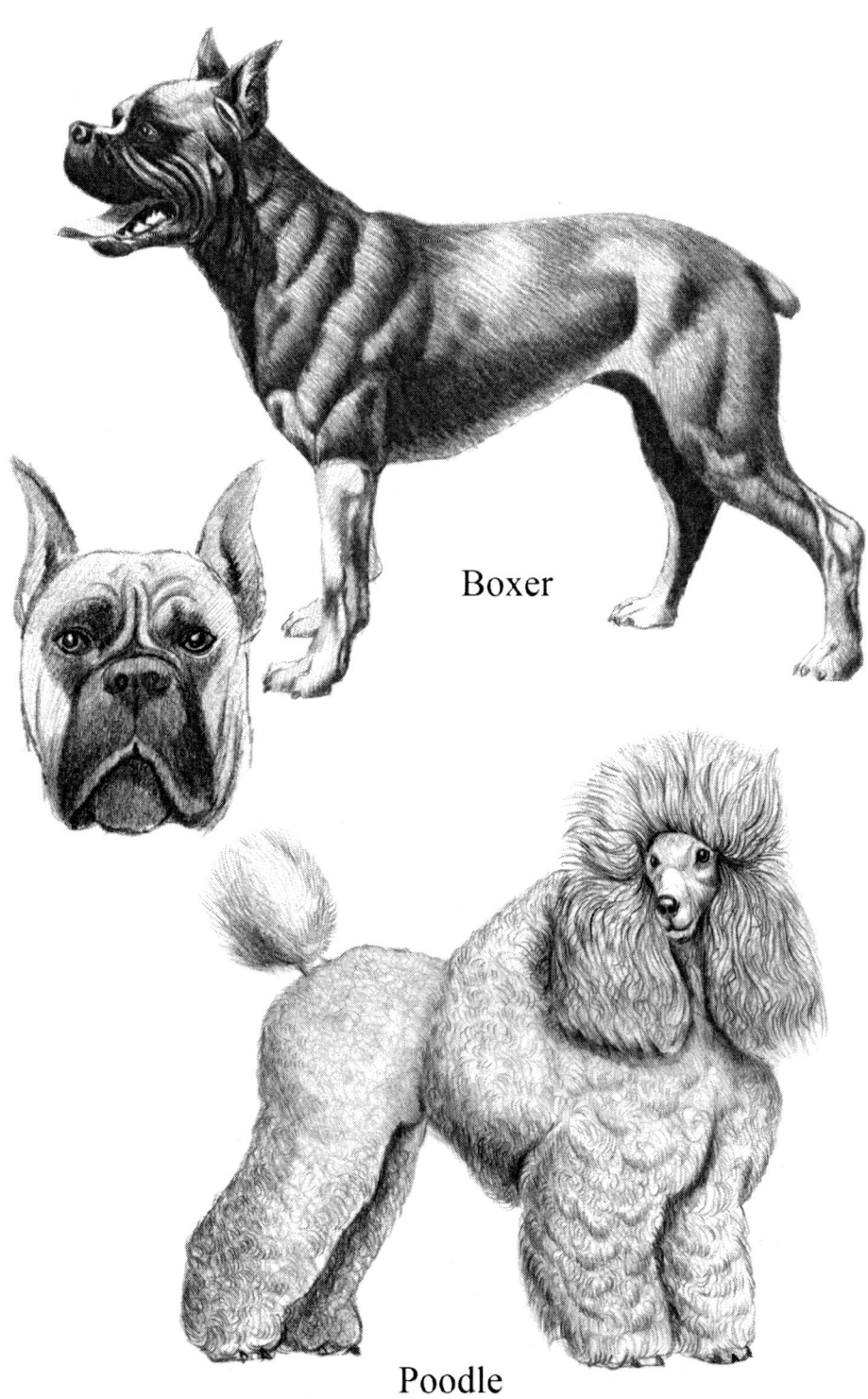

Boxer

Poodle

Brittany Spaniel

West Highland Terrier

Welsh Terrier

Sheltie

Papillon

CANCER THE CRAB
June 22 through July 23

Silver is your metal
Your stone is a pearl
Heather is your flower
Your color is sea green
You also like grays
Now let's look for a pup to brighten your days

If a large, hyper dog raced about your living room, Cancer, most of you would leap out of your shells, and grab the breakables. This dog is probably not the kind of dog you want in your home, but before we name the breeds with traits and temperaments that would interest you, it's important to us that you understand where we're coming from.

Initially, as a professional astrologer and a canine behaviorist, our first question was, "What kind of dog owner would a Cancer be?". We found the answer by thoroughly studying your sun sign personality. Once we knew what you would probably look for in a dog, we considered all of the breeds registered with the American Kennel Club to find some perfect pups for you. Now, we're not saying that you can only successfully own the dogs we have selected for you. What we are saying is that the pups we suggest would be good choices for your sun sign personality.

We'll first review the characteristics of your sun sign, and discuss dog traits and temperaments that could be a plus or a minus for you. Your compatible pups are then described in full so that you can make your own decision based upon your lifestyle and personal preference.

Your sign shows you to be an extremely sensitive person. You react to everything through your emotions. This makes you very vulnerable so most of you prefer to keep your feelings to yourself. You're a private person. Only a chosen few know what's really happening for you.

Because you feel things deeply, and do not often share your concerns with others, many of you agonize internally. On the surface you appear to be a casual and easy-going person. It's rarely apparent that you are worried about something, but in truth, you tend to worry quite a bit. Your active imagination doesn't help. It tends to make your problems larger than life.

Still, when a problem is solved, and you find that it was not as bad as you feared, you feel lighthearted, and have good reason to celebrate.

Many of you have a great sense of humor when things are right in your world. You have both wit and charm that makes your personality attractive to others. Because you think things through with your emotions, you are also intuitive. You often know where people are coming from without a great deal of explanation, and are a sympathetic listener. Some of you are empathetic. You are able to feel a friend's pain as though it were your own.

You love a little excitement in your life - something that's exhilarating, and gives you a chance to break out of your shell. Your enjoyment is greater if you can share those times, especially with someone special. In addition to being a social person, Cancer, you are also a romantic. To love and to be loved is all-important.

Your home is your harbor. Whether you live in a mansion or rent a room somewhere, you are usually happy to walk through that door. Your home is probably filled with all sorts of interesting things, dating back to year one. Every time you try to throw something away, your hand acts like a magnet, and you can't let it go. You probably have good memories attached to most of your things, and who throws good memories away? Not you, Cancer. All of your magic moments are special.

One of your favorite haunts is where water flows – salty or fresh. Many of you may be keen on water sports, and you like all kinds of boats. Walking on the beach, climbing the cliffs, wandering beside rivers and streams in the woods, and finding a cave to explore behind a waterfall is a favored way to spend your time. If you live in the city, a fountain in a city park will slow your step, even if you are late for an appointment. Water has a strong pull for you.

For most of you, a walk beside the water or a boat ride is fine to do alone, but you don't really want to be alone that much unless you are escaping from people who have caused you grief. You need someone close by who cares. Unfortunately, there are, and will be, times in your life when you do feel all alone. What could be a comfort to you at those times is the right kind of dog by your side. Your dog will penetrate your loneliness, help to bring you back into the world, and will always be there for you.

You'll adore your puppy no matter what breed it is. You nurture your loved ones with possessive pride. Still, it's a good idea to get one that will not let you down when it grows up. Let's take a look at the traits and temperaments that could be a minus or a plus for your personality.

There are times when you do not want to be bothered by anyone or anything, Cancer. You need your space. If you have a dog about that will not respect this, and constantly bugs you, most of you will blow a fuse. Some breeds are aloof, and will not demand much from you. In fact, they might not even be aware that you are there. But it's only at certain times that you want to be left alone. A lot of the time you'll ask a great deal from your dog and an aloof breed can't be relied upon to deliver. What you need, then, is an intuitive dog - one that tunes in to what's happening for you, and responds in the right way to all of your moods.

A pup from an aggressive, dominant breed will certainly respond to how you feel, as many of these dogs are intuitive – too intuitive! The pup would quickly learn when you have tuned out, and take full advantage of it to think and act on its own. Now most of you have an over-all attitude of live-and-let-live, but you can't apply this philosophy to an dominant breed. It would soon take over, and has the potential to give you quite a bad time. You'd be much happier with a dog that shares your home with you on your terms.

Intuitive, and able to respond to your way of doing things without a hassle sounds good, but some dogs have these traits along with an exuberant spirit, in and out of the home. Some of you collect things, and have had some of your possessions since childhood. They may not be seen as valuable to some, but to you, their sentimental value is beyond price. A large, happy, bouncy dog can do damage in your home without even trying. Of course, if you take it for a three-mile run daily, it will settle better indoors, but is that something you are likely to do? Once started, the dog will demand it, and most of you hate to be pushed into anything you don't want to do. A patient dog with good manners in the home would be much more compatible with your personality.

So far, your perfect pup should be intuitive, responsive to your needs, eager-to-please, and not from a dominant breed. It should be well behaved in the home, and not hyperactive. What if you got a pup, though, that fit these requirements, but hated getting wet? Maybe it's a city dog – a dog that considers sport to be something its owner watches on television. If you took this one camping, or out for the day by the water, it would probably sit on the bank shivering and whimpering. When you are at the beach, or on the river, many of you would enjoy a dog that splashes with the best of them – a dog that loves to do the same things that you do. A fun-loving, playful dog that loves the water, the beach, and the woods should now be added to your dog's preferred breed traits.

Of course, there are some of you who will want a less active dog – one that will appeal to your nurturing nature, and we have included some special Toy breeds for you for that reason.

Finally, Cancer, any dog you own should be both affectionate and loyal. Most of you have a strong need to be first with those you love. Your dog doesn't have to love everybody, but it should love you without reservation.

A pup that can grow up to be your true friend and companion is sure to win your heart, but once you have chosen the breed, you then have to pick the pup from a litter. To choose a good one, you should put that protective, nurturing nature of yours on hold for a moment or two. The pup that runs up to you, and chews on the laces of one of your favorite old sneakers is a good choice. If you see a pup peering at you from under its mother's legs, shy, timid, with big sad eyes, turn away! Scoop up the pup who has now started on the laces of your other shoe, and don't look back. This one will be more likely to be true to its traits and temperaments, and will need all of your tenderness when you get it back home.

You'll train your pup with pride and affection, Cancer. When the pup learns its lesson, you'll be delighted with its intelligence, and will probably hug it in addition to giving it a treat. Don't forget to allow the pup time to mature for bladder control, though. A pup's accidents in your home are not personal.

Give some thought to your lifestyle when you are considering the breeds suggested for your personality.

The first dog we suggest for you, Cancer, is a popular breed.

COLLIE – ROUGH AND SMOOTH
Colors: Sable and white, tricolor, blue merle
Height: 20"-24"
Weight: 40 – 65 lbs.

This Scottish sheepdog is intelligent and intuitive. It's well behaved in the home, and playful outside. A Collie has a very sensitive temperament akin to your own, Cancer, and will respond well to most of you. It will appreciate your hugs, but will stay clear of you when your voice is not warm and welcoming.

Because the breed is both intuitive and sensitive, any harsh handling of this pup would turn the dog timid. A firm voice is all that's needed to halt it in its tracks when it's headed the wrong way. When the pup does well, lots of praise will feed its spirit. It will try its best to please you, Cancer, as the dog will crave your approval once the attachment and bonding process has taken place.

The Rough Collie is considered to be easier going than the Smooth, but neither is aggressive unless they are protecting you or your property. Of course, you'll know the Rough Collie as Lad or Lassie, made famous through the movies. Although Lad and Lassie were specially trained canines, their stories portray just how bright and versatile Collies are, and how much they love their owners and their homes.

Rough Collies have beautiful coats but they shed. You should brush your dog regularly, starting as a pup. When you groom your pup, you are taking over where its mother left off, and letting the pup know who is now in charge. Brushing its coat with affection will also help to cement the growing bond between you. Smooth Collies also need regular brushing to keep the shine on their coats.

A well-groomed Rough Collie is more popular as a show dog, and the breed has taken the highest honors. If you intend to show your Collie, it will perform well for you. If you use a professional trainer for Show, make sure the dog knows and trusts the handler.

If you decide upon a Collie, you'll have a gem of a dog in your home. Collies are well mannered and move about quietly indoors. If you have china collectibles on low tables, though, you'd better move them. A happy Collie wags its long tail as a greeting. Outdoors, a healthy Collie bounds with joy. It's a playful dog, loves to roam the woods and fields, and is a wonderful outdoor companion.

If you are in the country, you may have to prevent your young dog from herding the neighbor's sheep. Its ancestors were good at that. In fact, its herding instincts are so strong that if it doesn't have sheep to herd, it will substitute. If you have children, your dog will watch over them like an anxious parent, herding them away from busy roads, the edges of cliffs, the banks of rivers, or rough seas. If you are the dog's sole responsibility, it will take care of you in the same way. It nurtures those it loves.

If you live with a group of people, or in a family, a Collie will be quite sociable with everyone in the home, but it will choose its special person quite early. That person will be the one who grooms it, feeds it, trains it, and takes it for walks.

When it comes to strangers, your Collie will be polite but reserved. It's a good idea to *socialize* a Collie pup when it's three months old. This is its special imprint time. Introduce the pup to friendly strangers and to other dogs in pleasant circumstances so that the dog will be more comfortable in crowds and at social gatherings for all of its life. This will not affect its ability to be a good watchdog.

The demand for Lassie dogs has resulted in some poor bloodlines, so check out your breeder before you contact him. And don't forget to choose the outgoing pup. Collie pups should be playful, spirited and friendly.

The next breed suggested for you, Cancer, is known as the game-keeper's dog.

FLAT-COAT RETRIEVER

Colors: Black, sometimes liver
Height: 22" - 23"
Weight: 60 - 70 lbs.

Newfoundlands bred with Setters probably produced Wavy-Coated Retrievers. It's thought that Wavy-Coats were then bred with Collies to give us Flat-Coats. The breed was developed in the 19th century to retrieve shot game. They are excellent gun and water dogs. Gamekeepers, who, by profession, demand a high performance level from their dogs, chose the breed as the best for the job.

Flat-Coats are a hardy breed, able to withstand the coldest of weathers and freezing water temperatures. They are tireless in the field, and since they retrieve naturally, they learn the rules quickly. Highly intelligent, eager to please, and responsive to their handlers, Flat-Coats are fine examples of a sporting breed.

If you don't hunt, this dog performs well at Field Trials and shows particularly well. Because it's a social breed, it has no problems with the hustle and bustle of the show world. It never hurts to *socialize* any pup, though. Introduce the pup to friendly people and other canines in pleasant circumstances at its special imprint time of three months.

Labradors and Golden Retrievers put Flat-Coats behind in popularity for a while, but the dog has made a comeback in recent years. This is not surprising as its breed traits and temperament are exceptional. What you will particularly like is that this one is easily trained to be a good housedog – sensible and quiet in the home. If you have children, your Flat-Coat will be good with them. It loves to romp and play, and ball games and fetching sticks are its favorite games.

Flat-Coats are watchdogs. They can treat visiting strangers with suspicion, but once they are sure that no harm is intended, they will become amiable. Your Flat-Coat is capable of great devotion and abiding faithfulness, Cancer, and its focus will be to protect you and your property.

Brush your pup regularly. Not only will the dog's coat shine, it will remind your pup it has a new boss now that its mother no longer grooms it. Flat-Coats love to be groomed and will stand quietly throughout, except for an occasional lick of appreciation.

It's hard to fault the Flat-Coat, but you should know that the dog has an additional ability to swimming, retrieving, and romping happily in the woods. It can also climb, and like everything else, does it very well. For some Flat-Coats, chain link fences and brick walls are not a challenge if there's a rabbit to chase on the other side of your enclosed yard.

A very similar breed is the **CURLY-COATED RETRIEVER.** The Flat-Coat has a glossy coat with feathering on its chest, belly, and tail, and on the back of its forelegs. The Curly-coat is thick with tiny curls that look a lot like astrakhan. Both breeds are beautiful proportioned, and if black, have dark brown eyes; liver-colored dogs have amber eyes.

A Poodle was added to the mix to get the Curly-Coat, and the breed was first registered with the AKC in 1924. The Curly-Coat can be more standoffish than the Flat-Coat, but both are steadfast dogs. This breed is popular in Australia for hunting duck in the swamps and lagoons of the Murray River. Little grooming is required for the Curly-Coat, but exercise is essential for both Curly-Coats and Flat-Coats.

Both of these retrievers love water, but if you live by a large expanse of water, this enormous, furry, cuddly dog is suggested for some you. Because of its size, and needs, it is not a dog many of you will choose, but because it is so special, we have included it for your sun sign personality.

NEWFOUNDLAND
Colors: Black, sometimes gold, gray
Height: 28" - 30"
Weight: 110 - 145 lbs

The Newfoundland is an enormous dog that loves water even more than most of you do. Its size does not make it aggressive. The Newf lumbers about like a gentle, dignified bear, calm in temperament and docile in the home.

Although authorities are sure the dog originated in Newfoundland, how exactly this breed came about is argued. Some Canadian authorities claim the dog stems from the big black bear dogs that the Vikings introduced in 1000 AD. Others say the Newfoundland came from the Great Pyrenees, taken to Newfoundland by Basque fisherman. The breed ended up in England where breeders developed the dog we know today.

It was a Newfoundland by the name of Seaman who accompanied Lewis and Clark in their expedition, and it's hard to forget the Newfoundland, Nana, who took care of the children in the original *Peter Pan* movie.

As a rescue dog, the Newf is quite famous, and has helped to rescue people from shipwrecks. Fishermen used their Newfoundland's strength to haul in their nets. The breed is still used in Labrador and Newfoundland as a hard working member of the team.

If you want your dog to compete, the Newf has no problems going to Show. It's good at cart racing, too

This dog trains well, but patience is needed. Like most large breeds, it grows out of its puppy stages slowly. When the pup is raised with lots of affection, and given time to develop, it's very loyal and totally devoted to its owner.

It's essential to live by the water to own a happy Newf. Swimming and diving is their favorite form of exercise. You'll have a built-in beach sitter for swimming youngsters. Newfs are very fond of the children in the family and tend to mother them. Of course, if you have a swimming pool, it would hard to keep your Newf out of it. This dog cannot resist any body of water.

As amiable as a Newfoundland is, it will show aggression if you, your home or your boat needs protecting. An owner of a Newf once told us, with amusement, that it's impossible to explain a boat sale to this dog. It will not permit the boat's new owners to board the boat. Since most of you resist getting rid of your favorite things, it's possible that your Newf will not have this problem to contend with. If you do decide to upgrade or downsize your boat, sell it to out-of-towners.

If you live in a hot climate, think twice before getting a Newf. Even though it sheds its thick coat in the summer, the dog is very uncomfortable in extreme heat. If you live in a cold climate, you'll have no problems. The Newfoundland has an extremely dense, thick coat, capable of handling freezing temperatures.

Needless to say, your Newf will need lots of brushing, especially at shedding time - spring and fall. During this time the dog will lose some of its rich color, but it will grow back. Some authorities recommend a dry shampoo for your dog over bathing.

A drawback to this breed for some of you, even if you live in a colder climate and by an expanse of water, is drooling. Due to its loose lip flaws, your Newf will drool and that's something you cannot train your dog not to do.

If you live in the right place for a Newf, and don't mind a bit of drool, its an incredible dog – one that some of you would totally adore.

A white dog with black markings known as the **LANDSEER** is similar to the Newfoundland in many ways, except that it is usually larger, and has curlier hair. This one is named for its breeder.

Obviously, Newfoundlands and Landseers are dogs only a few of you can own because of their size and lifestyle requirements, but if you love big dogs, here's one with lots of character and a wacky sense of humor.

OLD ENGLISH SHEEPDOG
Colors: White and gray, grizzle or blue
Height: 22" – 24"
Weight: 70 plus lbs.

The Old English loves its home as most of you do, Cancer, and rarely strays. Although it guards well, it's not usually an aggressive dog, and avoids getting into dogfights. You'll enjoy its sociable nature, particularly with children, and few breeds are as devoted to their owners as the Old English Sheepdog.

We should warn you, though, that this lovable dog is a grooming challenge. It loves to romp and play outdoors, and its coat is a mud and burr magnet. When this breed worked for a living guarding the shepherds' flocks, it was common practice to sheer the dog along with the sheep. Watch out for its coat matting, avoid metal combs, and if you want to show your dog, take it to a professional. This dog has shown very well, and has won Best with a grin on its face. If your sheepdog is not headed for the ring, bathe and brush regularly.

The dog's nickname is Bobtail, which comes from the usual practice of docking the Old English's tail very short. The breed originated in the West Country of England, but has become popular all over the world because of its very affectionate nature, intelligence, and responsiveness to its owner. In Australia and in the U.K. the dog is sometimes referred to as the Dulux dog, as it was used in the advertisements and commercials for Dulux paint. The breed's origins can be traced back to early 19th century, and it's thought by some that the Bearded Collie and the Russian Owtchar helped to create the breed.

Your Bobtail will guard you and your property. It once protected the flocks from wolves, and has retained its watchdog courage. Bobtails have a clearly recognizable bark, low pitched, but loud and ringing.

A one-person dog, the Bobtail prefers the company of its owner above all others. To help your dog to be more social, take the pup out and about at thee months old, the special imprint time for all pups, and encourage the fuss that strangers made over your adorable furry pet. This will help the dog to distinguish between friend and foe all of its life and will not affect its guarding abilities.

An Old English Sheepdog can live anywhere you do, town, country or the suburbs. It does not demand constant attention, but it does need daily exercise. If you don't have a fenced yard, you'll need to take the dog for nice long walks.

This one has a spirit that resists regimented training and mega rules and regulations. If pushed too hard, it could become stubborn, but who would understand this better than you, Cancer? You'll find that your Bobtail will obey cheerfully when trained in the right way. It obeys through its devotion to its owner, and most of you will have no problems winning this pup's very large and warm heart.

When people talk about their Bobtails, they grin a lot, but if you are looking for a less challenging, outstanding breed, this one may appeal to some of you.

GOLDEN RETRIEVER

Colors: Pale cream to gold
Height: 21.5" – 24"
Weight: 60 –75 lbs.

Some authorities claim that the Golden is a cross between Russian Sheepdogs and British Bloodhounds. One story goes an English breeder by the name of Lord Tweedmouth, who owned an estate on the Tweed River, purchased eight Russian sheepdogs in the mid-1800's. He bred them with bloodhounds to increase their scenting ability, and produced the Golden we know today. Another authority believes that Lord Tweedmouth mixed the local Tweed yellow water spaniel with an Irish Setter and English Bloodhound to achieve the Golden Retriever.

However this breed was achieved, the Golden Retriever is a beautiful dog with an intelligent, obedient, loyal and faithful nature. It's easy to train, and once the dog has been trained, it rarely forgets to stay on task. The Golden is a winner in Obedience, at Field Trials, as a guide dog for the blind, as an assist dog for the disabled, as a search and rescue dog, and in many other fields.

It's an excellent sporting breed, retrieving tirelessly from land or water regardless of weather conditions.

Although the dog works reliably in the worst of weathers, it's not good at weathering harsh treatment. A Golden has a sensitive nature and an overwhelming need to please its owner. It will certainly stay out of your way if you are not in a good mood. When it needs to bother you, the dog will gently paw your knee to attract your attention.

This dog is exceptionally popular, Cancer, because of its amiable temperament. It loves children, and is an excellent housedog. When neglected, and not given enough love and attention, though, the dog can go off its food and droop in spirit.

You'll need to brush your dog's longhaired coat often as it sheds. It's a good idea to start grooming your Golden when it's a pup. Make it a pleasant experience. The Golden loves to be brushed by a loving hand, and the bond between you will grow quickly.

This breed can be left at home alone, but be prepared for a big welcome when you come home, and a present. Your dog will grab the nearest thing to hand to give you. The trait is instilled from when hunters praised the dog for retrieving downed quail. If you don't want a closet filled with odd shoes, try keeping some of the dog's toys close to the front and back doors of your home.

Although the Golden is not an aggressive dog, it's still wise to *socialize* it at its special imprint time of twelve weeks by introducing it to as many strangers and other dogs as possible. Socialization will help your dog to be more comfortable in your absences in the care of strangers, and to be more confident in strange places for all of its life.

It really doesn't matter where you live if you own a Golden. The dog adapts to country. town and city life. It loves a romp on the beach, or in the woods. Exercise is important as it's a sporting breed, and it absolutely loves to go for walks. If you live near the ocean, and the dog plays in the salt water, be sure to hose off the salt at the end of the day to avoid dermatitis. Your Golden will love to travel with you by car also. Once your dog attaches to you, it wants to be wherever you are.

Few dogs can offer you the depth of devotion of a Golden, Cancer, and many of you will fall forever in love with this multi-purpose, talented dog. However, if some of you are looking for a smaller breed, the next breed suggested for your personality might be just what you are looking for.

BORDER TERRIER
Colors: Red, wheaten, grizzle and tan, blue and tan
Height: 11" - 15"
Weight: 12 – 20 lbs

The Border Terrier was developed on the borders of Scotland and England. They were not recognized as purebreds until 1920 in England, and 1930 in the U.S. They share an ancestry with Bedlington Terriers.

Some of you may remember the Border Terrier, Toto in the sequel to *The Wizard of Oz, Return to Oz,* or the one who played Hubble in *Good Boy* or Toots who was Lassie's co-star. Intelligent, bright little dogs, they have star quality, and have also taken top honors at Show.

Border pups are sensitive, which is why we think some of you would be good owners for this dog. If treated harshly, they can retreat into a bewildered silence, and hide. When handled without aggression, however, they blossom into wonderful little companions, full of fun and affection. Most of you have a special fondness for the small and vulnerable, and will quickly lose your heart to your Border Terrier pup.

Coat care for a Border needs special attention twice a year – spring and fall. In the spring its dense coat needs to be stripped ready for summer, and in the fall, stripped again so that it will grow in its heavier coat. You can take the dog to a professional for this, or you can be shown how it should be done. It's important to brush the dog regularly, too, which will increase the bonding between you.

Border Terriers will quickly adapt to your lifestyle. The dog will play happily in the yard, go on a ten-mile hike, or curl up indoors peacefully. You should *socialize* your pup at its special imprint time of three months by introducing it to as many friendly people and dogs as you can to help it overcome its shyness with strangers. Because it is small, this should be done with care or you will defeat your purpose

If you have a cat, your dog can be trained to adapt to its presence, but this won't go for your neighbor's cat. If you have hamsters or guinea pigs, you'd have a problem. To your Border, they are vermin to be dispatched immediately. In the 18th century, Border Terriers were expected to keep vermin down, and to provide for themselves. This made them very good hunters.

With the right handling, a Border pup will grow up to be devoted to you and to your family, and likes nothing better than sharing a home with good friends.

The next breed we suggest for you, Cancer is a popular Toy.

CHIHUAHUA – SMOOTH AND LONG COATS
Colors: Fawn, red, black and tan, various colors
Height: 6"-8"
Weight: Up to 6 lbs.

Mexico is considered the country of this breed. American breeders started their strains of dogs bought from the State of Chihuahua in northern Mexico. It is believed by some authorities that this breed is descended from Aztec dogs. Others believe that the breed is an import from the Orient. Some claim that a dog closely resembling the Chihuahua was kept as a pet in Egypt about 3,000 years ago. Debates continue on this Toy's origin. Certainly it is an old and favored breed, and is famous as a part of a Boticelli fresco in the Sistine Chapel in Rome.

This small dog has achieved fame in many areas. In the Guinness Book of World Records a Chihuahua named Boo Boo was listed as the smallest dog in the world in 2007, weighing in at one and a half pounds. A Chihuahua named Bruiser was Ellie Woods's dog in the movie *Legally Blonde*, and who can forget the commercials for Taco Bell? Chihuahuas have many other credits in books, for films, and in paintings. They consider Best in Show to be their due, and prance with delight when the judges agree with them.

Both the longhair and the shorthair varieties are popular, but the dog often at the top of the charts is the shorthair. It's a very clean pet, and requires no grooming. The longhair variety needs to be brushed gently and affectionately at least once a week.

This little dog will never willingly part with you, Cancer, and will protect you fiercely with every ounce of its few pounds weight for up to 20 years. Other people, though, are usually of zero importance. The Chihuahua doesn't care much for other breeds either. It will accept the company of another Chihuahua, which is why some owners buy a pair, and it often favors cats. Of course, since most cats are much bigger than this pup will ever be, it's more important that the cat likes the Chihuahua! If you own a cat, make sure you are there to make the introductions. Another animal that meets with a Chihuahua's approval is a rabbit. This is another turn-about, but then, nobody said this dog was ordinary in any way.

If you have small children, it's not wise to add a Chihuahua to the family until they are of school age. Chihuahuas, when frightened, can snap at small, grabbing fingers.

You'll need to get a cozy bed for your pup, and be sure to add a soft toy rabbit or cat for the pup to cuddle into. If the toys' eyes are plastic, remove them as they are a choking hazard. Keep a warm dog sweater in your closet also. If your small friend is a shorthair, it will need its coat when you take it out on a chilly day.

Chihuahuas are considered to be among the most intelligent of the Toy breeds, and despite their delicate appearance, they are quite hardy. You'll be tempted to baby this pup. It has large, expressive, luminous eyes that will show hurt for something as trivial as seeing you put its bag of treats back in the cupboard. A Chihuahua definitely takes everything you do personally. Train the dog as though it were larger, and refuse to go along with its bid for power. As amusing as this may seem to you, be warned that a pampered Chihuahua can be a tiny tyrant.

Mutual respect is important with this breed. Chihuahuas hate being laughed at. They have no idea why people scoff at them when they fiercely protect their owners, but those same people treat a Doberman or a German Shepherd with respect. Well, size is not a canine concept. Chihuahuas have no idea that they are a Toy breed. There is a great deal of pride and dignity wrapped up in this tiny package. After all, it has been owned by royalty, painted by the Masters, and adored by the masses for centuries. Most of you are not likely to laugh at your protector, though, Cancer. You will appreciate its loyalty and devotion, and many of you will treasure this one for all of its long life.

Here's a tip if you buy a Chihuahua, and then move. A Chihuahua we know couldn't find a spot in his new garden to relieve himself. His owner took our advice, and went back to his old house, and shoveled some dirt and rocks into a bag from the yard. He scattered the dirt and rocks in his new yard. The problem was solved.

Chihuahuas are wonderful Toy dogs, but here's another Toy breed that may interest some of you. It's definitely royalty.

PEKINGESE

Colors: Various – brindles, many shades
Height: 6"- 9"
Weight: 8 - 12 lbs.

History and legends abound when it comes to this 2000 year-old breed. One legend has it that a lion fell in love with a marmoset, and begged the patron saint of animals, Ah Chu, to reduce his size so he could marry. Ah Chu granted his wish and reduced his size to that of a pigmy, but allowed the lion to retain his great heart and his spirit. Another authority claims that it was Buddha that the lion went to for help, and this resulted in the dogs being sacred. Both legends result in the breed being called The Lion Dog of China.

The dog once lived in the Imperial Palace of Peking. It's said that the dogs were never allowed outside the gates, and should someone try to remove one, the penalty was death. In 1860, in retaliation for an offense against some western countries, military personnel stormed the palace. The members of court had fled, but five Pekingese were found. English officers took the little dogs home with them. They presented Queen Victoria with one, whom she named Looty. English breeders developed the breed recognized in 1906.

It was Dr. Heuston who brought the dogs to Ireland. The Chinese minister, Li Hung Chang, gave the doctor a pair of Pekingese as a gift for setting up smallpox vaccination clinics in China.

The dog found its way to the U.S. when the Dowager Empress Tsu Hsi gave Pekingese dogs as favored gifts to influential Americans.

Some well-known Pekingese were Sun Yat, a Titanic survivor, Munchu, Theodore Roosevelt's daughter's pet, and Penelope, the Philadelphia composer, Joseph Hallman's dog and, of course, Fifi, Pluto's girlfriend, was a Pekinese.

Although the Lion dog needs care when it comes to its coat, the dog is not in need of pampering generally. In fact, the breed is renowned for its courage and spirit. The Royal dog of China is well aware of its heritage, and prefers to be treated with respect. It will not make demands upon you, Cancer, if its needs are met. Your Peke will be off playing happily, looking for a cat to tease. This canine usually loves felines.

Once a week, you'll have to groom your dog with the right tools. The dog has a beautiful profuse coat which has a tendency to tangle and matt. You'll need to wash its face regularly, too, and bathe its eyes. The Peke loves to romp and play through the grass, but because it's low to the ground, it gets mud and grit in its eyes. City Pekes have less of a problem in this area.

As a show dog, the Peke has done exceptionally well, and has taken Best in Show, standing alongside some of the finest and noblest breeds in the world.

Living with small children is not good for a Peke – it does not do well with surprise grabs, and does not consider itself a stuffed toy.

Training should be done through affection and with the knowledge that this one has its own ideas about what it should be doing. Pushing a Peke into obedience creates a stubborn, snappy dog. That's not your way to do things, though Cancer. Your live-and-let-live attitude is just perfect for this one. Once it loves and trusts you, you'll find the dog's intelligence uncanny, and you will find it to be a faithful dog.

Collies, Flat-Coat Retriever, Newfoundland, Old English, Sheepdog, Golden Retriever, Border Terrier, Chihuahua, and Pekingese are the breeds suggested for your sun sign personality, Cancer. We hope we have been of help to you.

Good luck in picking the perfect pup.

Collie

Flat-Coat Retriever

Newfoundland

Old English Sheepdog

Golden Retriever

Border Terrier

Chihuahua

Pekingese

LEO THE LION
July 24 – August 23

Gold is your metal
Your stone is a ruby
Sunflower is your flower
And your color is yellow, sunny and bright
Now let's find the pup that'll be just right

When you are busy, doing some work at home that requires your total concentration, you would probably be behind a closed door. If you owned a dog that pawed at that door until the paint peeled off, you would blow several fuses. The dog's anxiety is not a breed temperament that most of you could admire. But before we get into the traits and temperaments that would be compatible with your Leo personality, it's important to us that you understand where we're coming from.

Initially, as a professional astrologer and a canine behaviorist, our first question was, "What kind of dog owner would a Leo be?". We found the answer by thoroughly studying your sun sign personality. Once we knew what you would probably look for in a dog, we considered all of the breeds registered with the American Kennel Club to find some perfect pups for you. Now, we're not saying that you can only successfully own the dogs we have selected for you. What we are saying is that the pups we suggest would be good choices for your sun sign personality.

We'll first review the characteristics of your sun sign, and discuss dog traits and temperaments that could be a plus or a minus for you. Your compatible pups are then described in full so that you can make your own decision based upon your lifestyle and personal preference.

Your sign shows you to be a person who is strong-willed and full of optimism. Most of you are ambitious. You undertake challenges with whole-hearted enthusiasm, overcome setbacks, and often win on long shots. In fact, Leo, you are a born leader.

Many of you have a radiant personality. There's not much that's luke-warm about you. People are drawn to you because of your positive energy, your charm, and your generous nature. In business, you will often lead them to success. On social occasions, you'll be in the center of the group that's having the most fun. Any exciting happening is sure to attract you, and you'll be a contributing force. In fact, you contribute your positive energy to most ventures. If there's a flicker of light, you'll fan it into a bright flame, Leo.

It's because you have a strong belief in yourself, and in your ideas, you do not hesitate to lead others. You rarely dilly-dally about, and you reject any negative input from co-workers, friends or relatives on your plans. Some of you have an incredible knack of getting to the crux of complicated issues quickly. You zoom in, spot the problem, and set about solving it. You don't often take the time to explain your actions, though, as you consider this to be a waste of your time. People, less enlightened, experience your wrath if they try to interfere. Some may call you arrogant, and this would bother you, but it wouldn't stop you.

You are intent on success, and sincere in your efforts. Most of you take a direct route in a straightforward manner. It's rare that you would stoop to be devious, and tend to judge others by your own behavior. This is where some of you get burned, Leo. People may go behind your back to sabotage you in the workplace. Personally, those you love and trust may also betray you. If such happenings occur you are not only confused, you are deeply hurt. Temporarily your lion's roar is reduced to a whimper.

Many of you enjoy teaching. It's rewarding to share concepts with eager students, and you make your classes interesting and exciting. Some of you have that intangible quality of charisma, and can hold your class's attention passed the dismissal bell. You can be impatient with those who will not use their talents, and seem intent on making a career out of failing, but you will try to turn them around. However, you will rarely tolerate rudeness from anyone or bad manners of any kind.

Rudeness is negative behavior and infuriates most of you. Before you lose your quick temper in public, though, you'll make your exit. When crossed at home, the sparks will fly. And that is just what your temper is, Leo. Angry sparks. Once inflamed, they die out quickly. Brooding about things is not your style, nor is going into the whys and wherefores of problems. You often forgive and forget as quickly as you flared up.

Pride is important to many of you. Pride in yourself, and in those for whom you are responsible. Because you also have a kind and compassionate nature, you'll give second chances, or even third to youngsters who may be having problems finding their way. However, you will expect results to be proud of eventually.

You'll consider your dog to be a part of your family, Leo, so it's more likely to win your affection if it's special in some way. Although you may feel compassion for unwanted canines, in truth you would not really want to own one.

You'll train the dog you choose with a firm, positive hand. At first its puppy antics will amuse you, and you'll play with the pup, but as it grows, your dog must show signs of meeting your expectations. Those expectations will vary with your lifestyle. If you hunt, you will want a dog that hunts superbly. If you need a protective breed, it must do its job well in guarding you and your family. If it's a show dog you are looking for, it should be able to win that ribbon. You like the best of things in all things, and this will include your dog.

To own a champion is a plus in itself, but let's take a look at the plus and minus traits and temperaments of certain breeds to help you to choose a dog that is a winner in more ways than one.

Your way of doing things is to use a direct, and quick approach. Many of you will respond well to a dog that can think fast on its feet. A dog that needs time to process your commands would soon irritate you. Even though the dog could be a champion show dog, its peculiarities would soon irritate you. An alert, intelligent breed, quick to follow your commands, would be of much more interest to most of you.

Now, although a bright, alert pup would be right for you, it should not be from a breed with a highly excitable temperament. You probably entertain quite a bit. If your dog joins in, uninvited, and bothers your guests, you should be able to dispatch it without ceremony. However, if you've chosen a dog that becomes very excitable when there are people about, it'll want to join in, invited or not. When you lunge for this dog, and knock over a tray of snacks or drinks in the process, some of your guests will love it, and grin at the dog, now trying to hide under the couch. It's not likely that you'll be amused, Leo. This dog has not only made a fool of you, unintentionally of course, but will probably do so again. A quieter, calmer temperament would be more compatible with your personality.

So far, Leo, the right breed for you should be bright, alert, and reasonably well behaved in your home, but what if you chose a dog that had these qualities, but attached itself to you like glue? Most of you will reign in your home. Your family belongs to you, and rarely is it the other way around. Over-possessive friends and relatives stifle you, so you probably wouldn't choose to own a possessive dog. Every time you turned around, this breed of dog would be under foot. Most of you dash about, always in a hurry. Yelling at this one wouldn't change its need to be by you. All you'd accomplish would be to make the dog slink about, hoping to get closer before you noticed. A less possessive, or non-intrusive dog would be better for most of you.

Of course, even though a dog that resembles clinging ivy is out, that doesn't mean you wouldn't want a pup from an affectionate breed. In public, you are not likely to baby or nurture your dog, but when you're alone, you will give it lots of affection, and be free with your hugs.

We are now getting closer to your perfect pup. However, a pup with all of the preferred traits and temperaments discussed above will not be a Leo dog if it looks ordinary. You love to own, or to be connected with, beautiful things - the unusual and the extraordinary appeals to you. A spectacular dog, or one that is unusual in an attractive way, would be the frosting on your cake.

To sum up, Leo, the right dog for you is a dog that's a source of pride, a winner in all ways. It should be intelligent, alert, well mannered, affectionate, and attractive. It should not be highly-strung, intrusive, anxious, over-possessive, or too ordinary looking.

The breeds suggested for your Leo personality suit various lifestyles. Some would be right for you, but not for where or how you live. Your lifestyle is an important consideration when making your choice.

The first breed suggested for you is unusual, and is outstanding as a protector.

RHODESIAN RIDGEBACK
Colors: Deep red wheaten, lighter wheaten.
Height: 24"- 27"
Weight: 65 - 85 lbs.

Since this dog is also known as the African Lion Dog, used for hunting down lions and keeping them at bay, we'd like to turn the tables here. You, Leo, will be in control of this magnificent dog, and you are the Lion sure to win.

The Ridgeback's distinguishing feature is the ridge of hair along its back running in the opposite direction to the rest of its coat. A native to South Africa, the breed was developed by Boer farmers. The Hottentots had a hunting dog with a ridge on his back, and this dog was mated with the settlers' dogs, which formed the breed we know today.

With its own family, the Ridgeback is a calm dog with clean habits and good manners. You won't have to groom this one a lot, but brushing the dog will help the bonding process between you. Bonding with your Ridgeback is vital from day one. When treated with respect, this dog is capable of great loyalty. It will protect you, your home, and your family from all intruders. Your strong, direct, but kind handling is the right way to go with this one Leo, but avoid training the pup when you're in a bad mood. It will not understand harsh treatment. The Ridgeback is highly intelligent and will seek your approval. Be sure to have treats on hand when the pup does well. Praise and treats work wonders.

Some breeders do not suggest getting a Ridgeback if you have young children. It does not tolerate careless and rough handling by youngsters.

The dog is definitely an aristocrat, and has a natural tendency to be aloof with strangers. *Socialize* your pup at its special imprint time of three months. Don't let this important time slip by and think you can do it later. It won't work later, and it's especially important for this particular pup. Socialization will help the dog to tolerate visitors to your home, and to be more relaxed when they are there. This will not in any way change its ability to guard you and yours.

Although Ridgebacks can be housed outside, able to withstand all sorts of weather, they would prefer to live indoors with you. Their primary need is to be your companion and protector.

Ridgebacks come with black noses or liver colored noses. The Ridgeback with the liver colored nose is often more playful than the more dignified black nose variety.

Recognition by the AKC took place in 1955, and Ridgebacks that have been socialized show well, and have taken top honors – well, if trained properly, the Ridgeback is always a winner, and a dog of which you can truly be proud.

Perhaps, though, some of you are looking for a furry bundle of charm. If so, check out this magnificent breed.

ALASKAN MALAMUTE

Colors: Shades of gray, sable, black or red, always with white.
Height: 23 - 25"
Weight: 75 - 85 lbs.

The Alaskan Malamute is from the Spitz group, and has been traced back to possibly 3,000 years, bred by the Mahlemuits tribe of Alaska. It has a long work history with man, and miners who came to Alaska during the gold rush of 1896 used the dogs to haul their rock debris away in wooden carts. Malamutes helped Admiral Richard Byrd to the South Pole, and Jack London and Rudyard Kipling focused upon the Malamute in their wonderful stories.

The breed has a similar disposition to you, Leo. It loves to be part of the action, is friendly, kind, high-spirited and definitely bold on occasion. It can also be quite dignified, observing the world through calm, proud, almond-shaped eyes.

The dog eats to meet its needs, its appetite varying according to how much exercise the dog gets. It's a strong and muscular dog that needs to run and play daily. For this reason, city apartments are not the best homes for Malamutes. They are quiet and well behaved in the home, but penning them up in small spaces really puts a strain on their robust natures.

If you live where it snows, your Malamute will be in its true element.

If cart trained, you can hitch the dog to a sled, and your dog will thoroughly enjoy pulling you and the kids through the snow.

The Malamute is a family dog, but this does not necessarily extend to other family pets. Some authorities believe that the Malamute was once bred with wolves, but whatever the reason, some Malamutes are not good with small animals, or at times with other dogs. *Socialize* your pup at its special imprint time of three months with as many dogs and people as you can in pleasant circumstances. This will help the dog and you, too!

Your dog will rarely bark, so it's not considered a watchdog. If you hear a wolf howling in the back yard, it's your Malamute. They also talk – sounding like Chewbacca in the *Star Wars* movies. Chewbacca's sounds are based upon a Malamute named Indiana, once owned by George Lucas.

You'll find the Malamute in hot climate states, but in truth, hot climates are hard on them. Their outer coats are thick and coarse, and under coats dense, oily, and wooly.

They shed their heavier coats in the summer, but there is no way to avoid the brushing your Malamute will need year round. Don't forget to give its tail a brush, too. It curls over its back like a question mark.

This breed is intuitive. If the dog senses that its owner is the indulgent type, it will surely take advantage. As a pup, it's absolutely adorable, and some find it hard to discipline this furry charmer, but discipline is just what it needs. Firmness with kindness is the way to go. You'll expect the dog to learn and to obey, and luckily for your Malamute, you usually give second chances. It will accept your leadership, but it's not naturally obedient. You have leadership qualities, and your Malamute can learn. Certainly Malamutes have done really well in Obedience, and star in the show ring.

When you walk your Malamute, be prepared for the fuss people will make when they see your dog. Few can walk passed this one without stopping to admire and appreciate how handsome this dog is.

The next breed suggested for you is known as the Apollo of Dogs, but is only for those of you who are willing to wait for over two years for it to grow out of its very large puppy stages. It does not reach full maturity until it is three, and unfortunately does not have a long life span – about eight years.

GREAT DANE
Colors: Fawn, blue, black, white, brindle, harlequin
Height: 22"-38"
Weight: 140 - 185 lbs.

Although its name implies that it comes from Denmark, and at one time that was probably so, this magnificent looking dog is now known as a

German breed. Its country of origin was changed during or after World War II.

Some authorities believe that the dog was bred from the Irish Wolfhound and the Old English Mastiff. Others think that Greyhounds and Tibetan Mastiffs went into the mix. It is also thought that the Bullenbeisser may be its ancestor. The breed is reported to be about 400 years old, but some sources claim that dogs similar to Great Danes were known in Ancient Egypt, Greece, and Rome.

Great Danes are famous in literature and film. It's not surprising to hear they made the Guinness Book of World Records for being the tallest dog. In 2004, a Great Dane from California named Gibson took the honors measuring 42.2" from the withers. Scooby-Doo, the Hanna-Barbera character was based on a Great Dane; Marmaduke was Brad Anderson's newspaper comic character; Butler was a fawn Dane owned by Captain James T. Kirk in *Star Trek*. Einstein was the Dane in Disney's *Oliver & Company*; Ace, the Dane from *Batman Beyond*; Mars and Jupiter were in *The Patriot*; Astro stars in *The Jetsons;* and Chester, Allan's dog is a Harlequin Dane in *Two and a Half Men*. The list of credits for the Great Dane is endless because it's just that kind of dog.

In the year 1870, Great Danes became Germany's national dog. Great Danes are also the state dogs for Pennsylvania.

Some of you will admire this dog's size, dignified bearing, natural elegance, and smooth, long stride. It's truly a giant among canines. Its color adds variations to its disposition. The heavier-set Harlequin Great Danes, which are white with black markings, are often more aloof than the bouncier fawn and brindle-colored dogs. Harlequins also have the reputation of being less eager to please. Black and Blue Great Danes can be standoffish, also, as compared with their fawn or brindle brothers and sisters.

You'll have a hard time convincing people that anything this big is still a pup when it's over a year old, but it's true. Because of their size, Great Danes do not start to mature until they are over two years old. How they are raised and trained in those two years is important. Your Great Dane needs a handler, such as yourself, to control it right from the start. Direct, firm and positive handling will ensure that your pup will reach its incredible potential. Punitive or harsh handling of this dog for the first two years would be a bad mistake to make.

Some members of this breed are a touch soppy, and you may get one that makes repeated attempts to be your lap dog. It will finally settle for leaning against your legs. You probably won't allow this for long, though. The dog's weight would surely restrict your blood circulation.

Great Danes have worked at many jobs – hunters, war dogs, and police dogs. Today they are guard dogs, show dogs, and companions.

A romp with children is highly favored by some members of this breed – the fawn or brindle variety – but unfortunately the young dogs often knock their playmates down. When trained and mature, this dog watches over its charges with indulgence.

The breed is fond of its own people, but it's not known to be friendly with strangers. Its guard dog traits dominate. If the dog is intended as a member of the family or for show, *socialize* the pup at round three to four months old, which is its special imprint time. Just make sure it meets and greets friendly adults, children, and other dogs in pleasant surroundings. This will help the dog to be more comfortable with visitors for all of its life, and will not affect its guarding abilities.

Cement the bonding process and your control over the pup by brushing its short coat. Regular brushing will keep its coat glossy. You should be the person who grooms, trains, feeds, and walks the pup. By taking care of the dog's needs, and always in control, you demonstrate that you are Alpha, the leader of its pack. The dog will then become obedient and very loyal to you.

It's unwise to get a Great Dane if you live in an apartment. The dog needs space to move about in, and becomes too territorial if restricted to small areas.

Great Danes are certainly awesome dogs if you can make the commitment, and spend the time working with the breed. Perhaps, though, you are looking for a sporting breed. If so, this one is spectacular.

WEIMARANER
Color: Gray
Height: 23"- 27"
Weight: 50 - 62 lbs.

The spirited, graceful Weimaraner has a nickname among sportsmen. They call it the *Gray Ghost*. In the fields at dusk, light reflects off its metallic coat, and its pale eyes shine. There's nothing ghostly about its performance, though. It's a superb gun dog and bird retriever.

There are several things that many of you will particularly like about this dog, Leo. Weimaraners train to the hunt much earlier than most hunting dogs, and they excel at tracking. If you're wondering how brave they are in unknown terrain, German hunters once used this breed to track down wild boar, and hold them at bay. The police recruit them for their intelligence and trainability, and they do well at show, especially in Obedience Trials. As companions, they are both protective and loyal.

Your strong personality and upbeat style of training is good for this breed, but if you want the best from your pup, don't train your pup on one of your bad days. Most Weimaraners are sensitive to their owner's moods and feelings. Lighten up when training, and use a positive approach. If you lose your cool too often, the pup will become confused. There'll be no confusion when it catches on and performs well, though. Your enthusiastic response will mean more to the pup than its reward treat.

Because Weimaraners have fine, soft coats, housing them outside in winter in most states is not possible. When on a hunt, though, weather is not a concern. The dog keeps warm by working hard. You won't have to spend much time grooming this one. Weimaraners do not shed, and keeping your pup clean is easy. In fact, some Weimaraners groom themselves, just like cats.

Although it's a fairly large breed, it adapts to apartment living well, so long as you give it enough exercise.

President Eisenhower's dog, Heidi, increased the breed's popularity. There was some indiscriminate breeding to meet the public's demand at that time. Nowadays it is easy to get a real purebred.

Weimaraners have the reputation of being good all-purpose dogs. The dog will strive to please you, Leo, when mutual trust has been achieved. The breed has enough spirit, intelligence, speed and style for even the most demanding among you.

Another sporting breed may be of interest to some of you, but you'd better make sure you get the right one.

ENGLISH SPRINGER SPANIEL
Colors: White with liver or black
Height: 18"- 20"
Weight: 42 - 50lbs.

It all depends upon what you plan for this particular breed, Leo. A field dog and a show dog are quite different, so be sure to check with the breeder what his or her English Springer Spaniels have been bred for.

This spaniel has appeared in paintings painted in the 1600's and it's possible that it is the ancestor of most of the spaniels around today. Show English Springer Spaniels have taken Best in Show several times – they are beautiful dogs.

Famous spaniels include Buster, the spaniel who was the arms and explosives search dog serving with the Duke of Wellington's Regiment in Iraq, finding hidden arsenals of weapons and explosives; Spot Fetcher is the pet of President George W. Bush. Millie Bush was its mother, the pet of former President George H.W. Bush.

The field spaniel is as enthusiastic about its pursuits as you are Leo. It 'springs' its quarry. The dog dashes forward, flushes, and waits for the shot. Quivering with excitement, it stays alert to retrieve. The breed is particularly popular for pheasant, but is also used for grouse and woodcock. A rabbit is not likely to escape your yard, either.

Springer Spaniels make wonderful additions to the family. It's an affectionate breed, and most Springers love to romp and play with children, the more the merrier, and will be fond of everyone in the household. It needs exercise, so walks and backyard play is essential. A Springer we know can make spectacular catches when thrown a tennis ball.

Socialize the pup when its three months old, the special imprint time for all pups, by taking it out to meet and greet men, women, children and other dogs in pleasant surroundings. This will help your spaniel not to be nervous around strangers for all of its life.

You should brush your pup's coat regularly, especially after a romp outside. A professional is advised to groom the dog for Show.

You will thoroughly enjoy teaching this one as it is eager to learn, and will seek your approval. However, even though the dog has an outgoing personality, it is sensitive. It does not do well with an aggressive, punitive trainer. The dog needs your enthusiasm, kindness, and affection to reach its potential. Some of you will bring out the best in this breed, and will own a dog that's a true champion.

The next dog is suggested for some of you because of its incredible beauty, grace and style. It's a very glamorous dog.

AFGHAN HOUND
Colors: Tan, black, fawn, cream, blue
Height: 24"- 29"
Weight: 52 - 62 lbs.

Because you have an innate understanding of royal behavior, many of you will admire and appreciate this aristocratic bred. The Afghan has been the King of Dogs for countless centuries. Drawings of them, looking exactly as they do today, have been found on rock carvings in Afghanistan, said to be 4,000 years old.

Famous Afghans include Rita from *Oliver and Company*, Sylvie from *Balto*, Brainy Barker from *Kypto the Superdog*, and it should be mentioned that Snuppy was the first dog ever to be cloned.

Afghans were once used to hunt gazelles. This is why, no matter how well trained your Afghan may be, it would be unwise to walk your dog without a leash, especially in the country. Some owners are still looking for their dogs that took off doing about forty miles an hour. Although this hound would enjoy the challenge a gazelle offers, the dog will chase any animal that runs-chickens, cats or rabbits.

On a leash, the Afghan is well behaved in the country, the suburbs or in the city, and there is a safe way to take off its leash, and watch your dog course. You can enter it in Lure Trials. Lure Trials simulate hunts for live game, and your Afghan would thoroughly enjoy the chase. It's exciting to watch the sight hounds course, and you would enjoy it almost as much as your dog.

At home, tthe Afghan will tolerate children quite well, and will allow petting with an almost indulgent expression. It is too used to being admired to actively crave attention. The dog usually stands quietly by its owner's side, or withdraws to its bed. It's not an intrusive breed.

Grooming is a must. You'll need a canine hairdryer and a pure bristle brush – this dog's coat is profuse. Make the effort to brush the dog yourself, Leo. It'll help with the connection you'll need to make, and the subsequent bonding such care brings. Needless to add, a professional would be needed if your Afghan were intended for Show. They are spectacular contestants in the show ring.

Some critics of this breed have accused the Afghan of being merely ornamental with a desire to please itself, but although the dog does not curry favor, if you play with your pup, you'll respond to its sweet nature.

Somewhat like a feline, this canine is not always obedient, but it's probably looking inward at the time, and has lost its focus. With your approval and kindness, you will soon develop a good relationship with your King of Dogs.

There are some of you that are interested in small dogs, or your lifestyle prohibits owning larger breeds. The next breed is presently famous for taking The Best in Show at Westminster in 2008.

BEAGLE
Colors: White with black and tan saddle markings.
Height: 13"- 16"
Weight: 18 - 30 lbs.

Originally an English hunting dog, the Beagle pack ran with the hounds. It hasn't forgotten foxes and other game are about for the chase, and enters into the whole business with quivering excitement. Well, the Beagle enters into most things in this way. It's a very happy, eager little dog with an optimistic outlook on life. This is probably why the breed has an excellent reputation for living to a ripe old age.

Instant obedience is just not one of the Beagle's best points. However, it's a very lovable, mischievous little dog with a very affectionate nature. If you raise the pup with a loving, firm hand, and win its loyalty, you'll also solve the obedience problem – well, most of the time.

You don't have to live in the country to have a happy Beagle. It's very adaptable, and good for the suburbs or apartment living. Of course, one of the first things it will learn is where you keep its leash, and will probably bring it to you the moment you walk in the door.

The Beagle's coat is short and smooth, but brushing the dog will help to keep it shiny. You should watch your dog's diet, though. The pup will soon learn who munches a lot in your family, and comes equipped with charming begging skills.

A Beagle is not hard to show because the dog's lively temperament and keen interest in everything that's going on helps it to show well. It loves to be part of a family, and is good with children. It also loves playmates of its own breed. Lyndon B Johnson owned three Beagles named Him, Her, and Edgar.

Most people who have owned Beagles stay faithful to the breed. It is trained through affection, returns the affection with devotion, and is usually lots of fun to live with. It will go wherever you go, Leo, and every outing will be viewed with extreme excitement. Some of you will absolutely adore this one.

Some breeders have a smaller version of this dog, under 13", and if your taste runs to Toy breeds, check out this one, also.

SHIH TZU
Colors: All
Height: 9"- 11"
Weight: 12 - 15 lbs.

The Shih Tzu once lived in the imperial palaces in China and was highly revered as a sacred breed. It is known as the "Little Lion" because it was clipped to look like one. The breed was first recognized in Britain in 1934 and came to the U.S. post World War II when military personnel brought the little dogs home with them. The AKC recognized this one in 1955, and the breed was not entered into championship shows until 1969. When a Shih Tzu won Best of Show at New Brunswick first time out, the American public noticed the breed, and it has since become immensely popular as a show dog and companion.

One of the things that will amuse and delight you about this dog, Leo, is that it demands respect, and needs to be shown it is an important member of the family. In your positive, kind hands, the dog will become convinced of its importance, and will happily settle in as an affectionate member of the household.

A Shih Tzu is a hardy, energetic little dog that will create games of its own with its toys if left alone, but would much prefer family members to play, too. The dog loves to be taken for a walk, and is eager to see the world outside its home.

In the summer, if you don't intend the dog for Show, take it to be clipped. Shorter hair would be more comfortable. You'll still need to brush out any debris the dog has picked up from playing outside.

When hot, the pup may gulp the water too quickly, so some owners buy a rabbit bottle for their Shih Tzu's. Licking their thirst away prevents water getting into their noses. Also, as with a toddler, you may need to wash the dog's face when it has finished its meal. A wet paper towel will do the trick. Sometimes they get their food into their eyes.

Most owners of Shi Tzus adore them, but if you are looking for a Toy without so much hair to deal with, and do not have small children, check out this one.

MINIATURE PINSCHER
Colors: Black, blue, brown – tan markings on face.
Height: 11"-12"
Weight: 7 – 9 lbs.

The Min Pin, as this one is affectionately called, is not a smaller version of a Doberman, as is sometimes assumed. The breed came from the German Smoothair Pinscher, and has been recognized since the 16th century. Some claim it has been around for much longer than that.

The dog is perfectly proportioned, agile, and has a very spirited temperament. It was once a ratter, and was very good at its job. Nowadays, the dog is an excellent watch dog, show dog, and friendly companion to adults.

Although the Min Pin only weighs a few pounds, nobody has informed the dog that it's a pint size. It behaves much like a larger dog, and has more courage than many of them. You'll need to take a firm and direct approach with this Toy, and, in a nice way, let the dog know who is the boss right from the start. It's quickly stimulated, and easily distracted, but it's also very intelligent, eager to please, and very affectionate.

In personality and behavior, it's a tough little dog, but in truth it's also fragile. This is why young children should not handle a Min Pin. They will unintentionally hurt the dog, and will teach the dog to fear them, and to snap at them.

The little dog is very energetic, and walks must be frequent if you don't have a back yard with a fence. If you do have a fence, you'll see your dog walking on its hind legs to check out something interesting happening on the other side. Unfortunately you can't let the dog off its leash on walks. It's a hunter at heart, and would take off without much thought to the dangers ahead. Recall is not its strong suit.

The dog tends to be over protective of its home and its owner, and it would be wise to show the pup that all strangers are not suspect. This is particularly important if you live in an apartment. *Socialize* your pup at its imprint time of three months so it is more comfortable with guests to your home, and friendlier to the neighbors. Because of its size, you must monitor the socialization. If strangers unintentionally hurt the dog, it will never believe you again.

Buy a cozy bed for this pup, and lots of toys – preferably not rubber or plastic as the pup will chew on them and could choke. Get the pup soft toys, balls; toys that run across the floor for the dog to chase. Browse through the cat toys *without catnip* in the pet store. While you are there, buy a coat for your dog if you live in a climate where the winters are cold.

The Miniature Pinscher is a wonderful little watchdog, and if handled properly, with firmness and affection, a loyal and loving friend.

The Rhodesian Ridgeback, Alaskan Malamute, Great Dane, Weimaraner, English Springer Spaniel, Afghan Hound, Beagle, Shih Tzu, and Miniature Pinscher are the breeds we suggest for your sun sign personality, Leo. We hope we have been of help to you.

Good luck in picking your perfect pup.

Rhodesian Ridgeback

Alaskan
Malamute

Great Dane

Weimaraner

English Springer Spaniel

Afghan Hound

Beagle

Shih Tzu

Miniature Pinscher

VIRGO THE VIRGIN
August 24 through September 23

Mercury is your metal
Your stone is sandy quartz
Bachelor's Buttons are your flowers
And your colors are shades of brown and blue
Now let's find that perfect pup for you

If you went to visit friends, Virgo, and saw their dog playing outside in the yard, you would probably say 'hi' to the dog. If it tore in to welcome you with great joy, and left mud on your jeans and on the sleeve of your shirt, your pleasant mood would change to one of irritation. A dog with a modicum of decorum would suit you much better. Before we go into which breed traits and temperaments would be compatible with your personality, though, it's important to us that you know where we're coming from.

Initially, as a professional astrologer and a canine behaviorist, our first question was, "What kind of dog owner would a Virgo be?". We found the answer by thoroughly studying your sun sign personality. Once we knew what you would probably look for in a dog, we considered all of the breeds registered with the American Kennel Club to find some perfect pups for you. Now, we're not saying that you can only successfully own the dogs we have selected for you. What we are saying is that the pups we suggest would be good choices for your sun sign personality.

We'll first review the characteristics of your sun sign, and discuss dog traits and temperaments that could be a plus or a minus for you. Your compatible pups are then described in full so that you can make your own decision based upon your lifestyle and personal preference.

The symbol of your sign, the Virgin, has nothing to do with whether you have ever had a partner. Virginity is the ancient symbol for purity, and is intended to show that Virgos are born to seek purity. Deep within many of you there is a great spirituality, which is your driving force to forever seek the true and honest path.

Your sun sign shows you to be a very discriminating person. You have both an inquiring and an analytical mind that rarely allows you to tolerate imperfection. It's not surprising then, that you do not often accept things at face value, nor do you act impulsively. Mistakes can happen if you do. Most of you hate making even small mistakes. Checking out things and thinking about them carefully helps you to avoid them.

Because of your own integrity, you are constantly seeking truths. Since truths are usually based on people's perceptions of them, it's not often that you'll find someone who will see truths as you do. This leads to some disappointments, especially with your close relationships.

Close relationships are not easy for some of you. You are shy at times. It's a part of your reserved personality. In addition, feelings are not logical or rational, and this can put you at odds with yourself. You can be quite sentimental, but your blueprints get blurred when your heart starts to rule. To regain control, you may act in an abrupt way, even coldly, to achieve a sense of order. Those who do not know you well often misunderstand this. Once you feel more stable, you'll listen to your heart. When you love someone, your gentler self emerges.

When your deeper feelings are not involved, some of you relax, and look for fun times. Ruled by Mercury, you have a quick mind, and an easy way with words. You can also be a versatile companion as most of you are interested in many different kinds of activities.

A constant in your life is your strong sense of morality. You are concerned about the rightness of things. If you hear about people really down on their luck, you'll welcome the chance to help them in your own practical way. You can be counted on to come through, too. Most of you are very reliable.

Both in your business and private affairs, you not only want to know the facts. you want details. If there are figures involved, you'll often nitpick at the statistics until you get to your own bottom line. Other points of view interest you, but will not change your own view unless based on sound deductions. Most of you prefer a proven way to do things, and go by the book. This does not mean that you are a plodder, Virgo. In fact, that no frills attitude of yours often reduces unnecessary steps, and saves time. Time is important to most of you. There are few slackers who are Virgos. Using time to get the job done efficiently is time well spent.

Some of you are extremely neat in your appearance. You dress quite conservatively unless you are with a flashier crowd. Then you'll do your best to fit in. You don't usually want to draw attention to yourself.

What to wear is one of the things you worry about, as you prefer to be dressed correctly for any occasion. You also worry about being on time, and whether you have the right directions. The wrong ones could make you late. In fact, Virgo, you worry about a lot of things, but it's only apparent by the quick movements and gestures you make. Many of you look quite serene even if your stomach is doing flip-flops.

Your attention to even minor details colors every aspect of your life.

You usually try your best to do it right. It's possible that some of you miss the overall beauty of things because you tend to dissect and analyze each and every part.

The main characteristics of your sun sign personality indicate that, as a dog owner, you'll be demanding and exacting, but you'll also be very affectionate. Getting the right dog is really important for most of you. When you want to kick back and relax, it would be great to share those times with a reliable canine buddy. Some dogs could turn your relaxation times into tension-filled chaos, though, so let's take a look at what could be a minus or plus breed traits and temperaments for your Virgo personality.

Because most of you are down-to-earth folk, you would probably prefer a dog that looks like most people's idea of a dog. There are certainly some odd-looking dogs in the world, and they would intrigue you, but most of you would probably not want to own one.

While it's true that your set of blueprints will differ on what your own dog should be, most of you will want a dog that earns its room and board. Even though you will become fond of any dog you own, most of you would prefer a dog that contributes to your life in a practical way.

It's doubtful that many of you will allow your dog to curl up on your couches, or beg food from the table. At private times, though, you'll probably share snacks, and sit on the floor with your dog to give it a big hug. From day-to-day, though, your dog should exhibit good behavior or it just won't measure up for you.

While most of you will be indulgent with a puppy, you will expect a lot from an adult dog, and you will probably be conscientious in the pup's training. If the dog doesn't obey you, most of you will take its failure as partly your fault, and work harder with it. There are dogs, though, Virgo that you could train from dawn to sunset, and they still couldn't be guaranteed to obey. Their obedience would depend upon how independent they are, the amount of stimulation present, or how much they want to please you. These dogs are just being themselves, but most of you will take the disobedience personally. If the dog takes off at high speed in the opposite direction when you call, it will infuriate you. It would be better to get a pup from a breed that will recognize the needs of its owner above its own.

Some of you will flinch from a messy, smelly dog. Even though you may have given it a bath the day before, it has found mud puddles to romp in, and is delighted with itself. Although you'll appreciate this dog's affectionate temperament, bouncy spirit, and protective traits, you just won't be able to take its robust nature. When the dog brushes by your tan and cream couch and leaves muddy marks, you'll groan aloud. This dog is not for most of you, Virgo. A pup with a modicum of decorum would suit you better.

The cool, well-behaved, aloof breeds may be very attractive to some of you, but your inner nature really needs a dog that will love you with devotion. When several things have gone wrong with your day, and you are not in the mood to even think about them, a loyal and loving dog by your side could make you feel a whole lot better.

Well, so far we have regular looking breeds, dogs that contribute, are obedient, well behaved, and do not have an independent spirit. Robust, hairy dogs are out, as are aloof breeds. This narrows down the list considerably, but a perfect pup is only perfect in the eyes of its Virgo owner, as most of you would point out.

We agree with you, but although this truth is evidenced by your sign's characteristics, it is also true that you are capable of compassion. If your dog meets you halfway, you'll forgive a flaw or two. In your logical way you'll judge your dog on its merits, and be aware of where it falls short. Most of you will make a few adjustments in your canine blueprints for a pup that has stolen your heart.

When you are considering the pups we suggest, please consider your lifestyle also. For example, the first breed suggested for you would be more suited to the country or suburbs.

LABRADOR RETRIEVER
Colors: Black, chocolate, yellow
Height: 21"- 24"
Weight: 55 - 80 lbs.

Of all the sporting breeds in the U.S., Labrador Retrievers are undoubtedly the most popular breed. For those of you who want that verified, its popularity is noted by registered ownership with the AKC. It's truly an exceptional dog. As a pup, it strives to please, and should delight even the most demanding amongst you. Highly intelligent, easily trained, and capable of great devotion, the Labrador Retriever definitely qualifies as one of mankind's best friends.

Originally Labs were bred on the island of Newfoundland, which is now a province of Newfoundland and Labrador, Canada. Some authorities claim that the dog was once named the St. John's dog, used to help the fisherman in the St. John's area of Newfoundland. Others say that the Newfoundland dog was the St. John's dog, but the Labrador definitely has a Newfoundland in its mix. The British are credited with developing the breed we know today.

This dog's talents cover a broad range. The breed is used for hunting, tracking, retrieving, police work, search and rescue, guide dogs, aids for the disabled, and excel at agility obedience. It would be impossible to name all the famous Labradors, but to prove our point, Jake was a national canine hero searching and rescuing survivors of 9/11. He was also called into service for Hurricane Katrina victims. Lucky and Flo are counterfeit dogs, and sniffed out nearly 2 million pirated counterfeit DVD's. Buddy and Seamus are good friends of former President, Bill Clinton, and Russian President Vladimir Putin's has a Lab named Koni. Endal, a British Lab is the most photographed Lab. Among other things, Endal was the first dog to ride on the London Eye, and the first dog known to work an ATM. Reportedly, they are making a film about Endal's exploits into fame. Rascal was the first chocolate Lab to win the National Field Trial Championship, and you probably know Bouncer in *Neighbors*, and Luath in *The Incredible Journey*. The Canadian football team, the Memphis Mad Dogs had a Lab as their mascot.

If you are looking for a hunting dog, this one is tireless in the field and excellent in water. It ignores bad weather conditions, and has an obvious love of the sport. If you do not hunt, your dog might do some hunting on its own. Our Lab, Hector, often brought us a live pheasant or a duck when we were out walking in the fields. Carried in his soft mouth, the birds were complaining, but unharmed. Hector could also be counted on to bring us the children's escaped guinea pigs and hamsters that only he could find, and they were always unharmed when he dropped them into the children's laps.

Retrieving something, anything, and bringing it to you is often the way this dog shows its love for you. When you come home, your Lab will probably bring you a present. Now this could be anything within its reach, maybe a shoe, a hat, glove or a sock, and it will be presented to you with barely-contained joy. This is its natural behavior and comes from when its hunter owner praised the dog for retrieving downed birds. A retriever should not be scolded for being itself. If you'd like to keep your shoes, gloves or socks in pairs, keep a couple of the dog's toys by the front and back doors. Your dog will present those to you quite happily as your welcome-home gift.

The bond between you will grow quickly, and the pup will scamper after you from room to room. The pup needs to attach, and it will develop well with an affectionate and companionable owner. Left too much on its own, without human companionship, it could become depressed, and then positively mournful if things did not improve.

Children and Labs get along very well, and the dog likes most adults. They can be quite choosy about being friends with just any dog, though, and can be aggressive to visiting canines. *Socialize* your pup at its special imprint time of three months with as many friendly adults, children and other dogs as you can in pleasant surroundings. This will help the dog to be less suspicious of strangers to your home, but will not affect its watchdog traits.

Your firmness, along with your affection, is needed to keep this lovable dog under control. Training with physical punishment is not necessary. The tone of your voice works wonders with this one. Labs are proud to please their owners. When the pup does well, be sure to give it a dog treat along with your praise.

Exercise is important, as well as a fenced yard. Grooming its coat is not difficult, a brush with a good bristle brush should do it, but if you live by the ocean, and the dog is constantly in the water, wash off the salty water at the end of the day to avoid dermatitis.

If you remember that puppy stages last longer in larger breeds, a Lab can be everything you want in a dog. It will turn inside out to please you and rarely, if ever, let you down.

The next breed discussed for your interest has an equally devoted following.

GOLDEN RETRIEVER
Colors: Pale cream to gold
Height: 21.5" – 24"
Weight: 60 – 75 lbs.

Some authorities claim that the Golden is a cross between Russian Sheepdogs and British Bloodhounds. One story goes an English breeder by the name of Lord Tweedmouth, who owned an estate on the Tweed River, purchased eight Russian sheepdogs in the mid 1800's. He bred them with bloodhounds to increase their scenting ability, and produced the Golden we know today. Another authority believes that Lord Tweedmouth, mixed the local Tweed yellow water spaniel with an Irish Setter and English Bloodhound to achieve the Golden Retriever.

However this breed was achieved, the Golden Retriever is a beautiful dog with an intelligent, obedient, loyal and faithful nature. It's easy to train, and once the dog has been trained, it rarely forgets to stay on task. The Golden is a winner in Obedience, at Field Trials, as a guide dog for the blind, as an assist dog for the disabled, as a search and rescue dog, and in many other fields.

It's an excellent sporting breed, retrieving tirelessly from land or water regardless of weather conditions. Although the dog works reliably in the worst of weathers, it's not good at weathering harsh treatment. A Golden has a sensitive nature and an overwhelming need to please its owner. It will certainly stay out of your way if you are not in a good mood. When it needs to bother you, the dog will gently paw your knee to attract your attention.

This dog is exceptionally popular, Virgo, because of its amiable temperament. It loves children, and is an excellent housedog. Why we think it would be a good dog for you is because this is a dog that needs an owner who will truly appreciate the dog. When neglected, and not given enough love and attention, the dog can go off its food and droop in spirit.

You'll need to brush your dog's coat often, as it does shed. It's a good idea to start grooming your Golden when it's just a pup. Make it a pleasant experience. They love to be brushed by a loving hand, and the bond between you will grow quickly. Apollo, a Golden in our family, loved being sung to, so if you like to sing, Virgo, play music softly, and sing a song to your pup as you groom.

This breed can be left at home alone, but be prepared for a big welcome when you come home, and a present. Your dog will grab the nearest thing to hand to give you. The trait is instilled from when hunters praised the dog for retrieving downed quail. If you don't want a closet filled with odd shoes, try keeping some of the dog's toys close to the front and back doors of your home.

Although the Golden is not an aggressive dog, it's still wise to *socialize* it at its special imprint time of twelve weeks by introducing it to as many strangers and other dogs as possible. Socialization will help your dog to be more comfortable in your absences in the care of strangers, and to be more confident in strange places for all of its life.

It really doesn't matter where you live if you own a Golden. The dog adapts to country town and city life. It loves a romp on the beach, or in the woods. Exercise is important as it's a sporting breed, and it absolutely loves to go for walks. If you live near the ocean, and the dog plays in the salt water, be sure to hose off the salt at the end of the day to avoid dermatitis. Your Golden will love to travel with you by car also, and is up for anything you have in mind. Once your dog attaches to you, it wants to be wherever you are.

Few dogs can offer you the depth of devotion of a Golden, Virgo, and many of you will fall forever in love with this multi-purpose, talented dog. However, the next breed is also special in its own way.

GORDON SETTER
Colors: Black and tan
Height: 22"- 25"
Weight: 55 – 75 lbs.

The Gordon Setter is more stockily built than its cousins the English and Irish Setters, and has a calmer temperament. The fourth Duke of Gordon favored the black and tan setters and bred them for bird hunting in his native Scotland early in the 19th century.

George Blunt and Daniel Webster brought the breed to the U.S. in 1842, and the AKC officially recognized it in 1892.

In the field, the Gordon's work style is similar to yours, Virgo, in that it's dependable and methodical. The dog is renowned for its scenting ability and endurance. However, you should know that you cannot start to train this one for the hunt until it is at least eighteen months, and the dog will not be fully mature until it's three. Although the breed needs lots of exercise, be careful not to over extend the dog when young. It might cause joint problems in later years.

Gordon's are good family dogs, but can be too exuberant with young children. As a pup it has lots of energy, and this will remain into old age. Your Gordon would be sensitive and empathic, eager to please you in every way. It has a strong protective instinct, and will need your firm, but affectionate training right from the start.

The dog is intelligent and learns its lessons well. By six months, the dog will have chosen its primary person. Of course, if you want the primary person in your Gordon's life to be you, it must be you that feeds the dog, brushes its silky coat, walks it, and trains it. Then you will become Alpha – the leader of its pack.

Gordon Setters are protective. *Socialize* this sweet pup at about 3 months, which is its special imprint time. Take the dog out to meet, and be petted by strangers and children. Introduce the pup to friendly dogs. It will help your dog to be more relaxed when strangers are about, but it will not affect its ability to watch over you and yours.

A Gordon Setter's coat is not as long or as profuse as some, but it requires trimming and brushing. Grooming your pup is an excellent way to attach, Virgo. The dog will respond to your careful, affectionate manner, and will appreciate that you are removing burrs and tangles from its silky coat. If you want to show your dog, a professional is advised.

The country or the suburbs are good places to live for this one, although the dog does behave well enough to live in an apartment. The city is not advised, as concrete sidewalks do not have the scents this dog is born to track. If you have a backyard, it should be fenced. Your Gordon setter may decide to take off to look for you, or follow a scent it picks up in the wind.

Labradors, Golden Retrievers and Gordon Setters are wonderful sporting dogs, loyal, and devoted to their owners, but perhaps you are looking for a fine, furry watchdog. If so, this one may interest you.

NORWEGIAN ELKHOUND

Colors: Shades of gray
Height: 18" - 21"
Weight: 44 - 54 lbs.

Over six centuries ago, the Vikings used this Spitz breed as hunting dogs, and they are still used to hunt in Scandinavia. Descended from the wolf family, they excelled in hunting elk and bear. Types of this breed also worked on farms herding sheep, and guarding the inhabitants from wolf or bear attacks. They were brought to England in the late 1800's. The AKC recognized them in 1913, and they soon became popular as show dogs, police dogs, guard dogs and pets in the U.S. President Hoover was very fond of his Elkhound, Weejie.

As a pet, the Norwegian Elkhound soon becomes a treasured member of the family. It's a very clean dog in its habits, and even when wet, has little doggy odor. If you have gained the dog's trust, it's affectionate. You'll respond well to its intelligence, and to its eagerness to learn, Virgo, and your dog will walk quietly by your side without a leash. Of course, if the dog sees something threatening to you, it may dart to protect. This Elkhound is a diligent worker, and takes its job of guarding you quite seriously.

The dog is extremely hardy, muscular, and strong. It also has a highly developed sense of smell. It gives an excited bark when it scents, and then calls to its owner by sharper barks. The dog will use various cadences of its bark to communicate with you, and you are soon able to tell if the dog is on guard against intruders, or if friendly visitors have stopped by. *If verbally communicative dogs bother you, Virgo, you won't be able to untrain this trait, and should not consider the breed.*

The Elkhound's coat is very thick and dense. It will shed, and a good brushing is advised on a regular basis. Brushing the dog yourself in your deliberate manner is not only an excellent way to bond with your dog; it will also help to establish your dominance. The pup's mother once had this job, and the pup surely remembers when she was in control. This Elkhound needs firm and quiet handling, along with affection.

People respond well to this furry charmer, and the pup will be admired. You should *socialize* the pup at three months, which is its special imprint time, with as many friendly people, children and dogs as possible in pleasant surroundings. This will help the dog to be less wary of strangers to your home, but it will not affect its intense guarding abilities.

The dog needs exercise, as it is an energetic breed. If you ride a bike, your Elkhound will happily run after you for miles in a safe area, and would love to accompany you on long walks in the country. If you live where there is snow, your Elkhound will be in its true element. Hot climates are not the best for this one.

As a pup, it's an adorable bundle of fur, and as an adult, the dog will certainly justify the pride you will undoubtedly feel. However, some of you may have your heart set on a terrier breed, and if so, this one is the King.

AIREDALE
Colors: Black with tan
Height: 21"- 24"
Weight: 40 - 55 lbs.

Airedales hail from Yorkshire, the north of England, and it's said that its birthplace was the Aire Valley. Local otter hunters who wanted hunting dogs who were also large enough to protect the home developed the breed in the mid 19th century. It's a descendant of the Black and Tan, has the blood of the Otter Hound, and possibly the Irish Terrier. Some authorities claim that the Welsh Terrier is also in its mix.

Airedale Terriers are bold enough to have been used for hunting large game in Africa, India, Canada, and in America. In Europe they have been war dogs, on duty as messengers and guards. The police also recruit them.

Three Presidents of the U.S. owned Airedales – Theodore Roosevelt, Calvin Coolidge and Warren Harding, and you probably know that John Wayne never went anywhere without his Airedale, Little Duke. In fact, they called the pair Big Duke and Little Duke, and this is probably, where John Wayne got his nickname.

Whoever owns an Airedale and trains the dog is very significant. This breed does well with a firm and an affectionate hand, but people prone to excited outbursts will add stimulus to a dog normally stimulated by the world in general. We think you would be good owners for the King of Terriers, Virgo, because you are calm, deliberate, firm, but also affectionate. The King needs this type of handling to reach its incredible potential.

The Airedale's coat looks short, but it still needs grooming. To keep its smart appearance, a daily brush is necessary, and its coat also needs to be stripped at shedding time. If you intend the dog for Show, a professional is advised. Airedales show well, and have an alert performance in the ring. If *socialized* they do well.

Socialize your Airedale pup at its special imprint time of three months. Introduce the pup to as many people, children and dogs as you can find in pleasant surroundings. The dog will still probably be wary of strangers, but it will help when they come to your home. *Socialization* will not affect its guarding abilities.

You must exercise vigilance where this dog's aggression is concerned. It should not be in control of how it behaves or what it does. You must establish yourself as Alpha – the leader of its pack, but always with firmness and kindness. Punitive measures are always a mistake.

There's something you should know about Airedales, Virgo. Bold enough to face down a bear, some members of this breed are terrified by storms. When thunder rolls and lightning flashes, you will find some of these kings shivering under the bed. Fireworks have similarly affected some members of the breed. Nobody knows exactly why this occurs with some Airedales, but the dog should be reassured and soothed, and not punished for something over which is has no control.

If a terrier's spirit attracts you, but you would prefer a less demanding breed, check out this one.

SEALYHAM TERRIER
Colors: White
Height: 10.5"
Weight: 21 – 24 lbs.

The Sealyham is a Welsh Terrier, which has a small, but loyal following in the U.S. This may increase, however, because Hildago at Goodspice won the 2008 AKC Eukanuba National Championship for Best in Show. Actually, the Sealyham is a superb show dog, and has taken Best in Show at Westminster on four occasions

If you remember the movie *The Birds*, you'll have seen two Sealyham Terriers, Geoffrey and Stanley, being walked by Hitchcock in his cameo performance in the film. Hitchcock loved the breed, and actually owned three of the terriers, the third one being Mr. Jenkins.

Lots of well-known breeds went into the mix to develop this outstanding little dog – the Dandie Dinmont, Pembroke Welsh Corgi, Wirehaired Fox Terrier, and the West Highland White. It's a friendly little dog that is devoted and loyal to its family. Unlike some terriers, the Sealyham has a relaxed and calm disposition. It has a big dog bark, which makes it an excellent watchdog, and its outgoing personality and playfulness makes it a good dog for children.

Although the dog has spirit, it's usually quiet in the home, and even has a modicum of decorum outside. Of course, if there's game about, the Sealyham remembers its ancestral training, and it will probably quarry a fox or badger for you if it gets the chance.

One of the things you will like about this easy-going little dog, Virgo, is its behavioral consistency. You'll be able to rely on your terrier's temperament staying much the same all of its life. You can't push this one, though. Some authorities claim that a contribution from a Flanders Basset Hound in its breeding is probably responsible for its resistance to instant obedience through a quick-training program. The firm and controlled way you will train will be good for a Sealyham. Certainly your indulgence to sweet young pups is just what this one needs. When a Sealyham trusts and loves you, it will obey through its devotion to you.

It's important not to tease a Sealyham pup, especially with its food or toys. If the pup thinks its things are not safe, it might start to guard them. If your pup has something it shouldn't have, you could try swapping it with its own toy to gain its trust. Don't give it an ice-cube to lick on in hot weather, though. You'll never be able to explain to the dog what happened to that treasure!

The Sealyham's coat is long, and will require some trimming and grooming to maintain the dog's neat appearance. No self-respecting Sealyham can stand looking a mess. Grooming your pup will help to build a closer bonding between you.

Socialize your pup at its special imprint time of three months with as many friendly adults, children and dogs as you can find in pleasant surroundings. This will help your watchdog to be more relaxed when strangers are in your home, but will not affect its guarding traits.

The dog has the capacity to be lively, active and friendly if handled in the right way. Some of you will win this courageous small dog's heart just as it will certainly steal yours.

The next breed that might appeal to some of you is quite popular for all of the right reasons.

SCHNAUZERS: Giant, Standard, Miniature
Colors: Black, various shades of white-gray-black – silver for the **Miniature.**
Height: **Giant** 25.5"- 27.5", **Standard** 18"- 20" **Miniature** 12"-14"
Weight: **Giant** 70 -75 lbs. **Standard** 30 -34 lbs. **Miniature** 13 -15 lbs.

Schnauzers are German in origin. Schnauze means muzzle in German. It's thought by some that there is some Old English Terrier in their breeding and possibly some German Affenpinscher, and Wolf Spitz. Some authorities think that the black German Poodle was also in the mix. The breed was once known as the Stable Griffon because the dogs accompanied stagecoaches on long, overland journeys as both guard dogs and companions. It's a breed with highly developed senses, and is noted for its bravery, intelligence, and devotion to its owner.

The Giant, Standard, and Miniature are very much alike in character. They are all feisty, protective, loyal dogs. The police and the military recruit the Giant. It's too large for apartment living, but the other two adapt well to this lifestyle if they get enough exercise. The Miniature Schnauzer is easy to train because of its intelligence, and willingness to please. This one has gained distinction in Obedience.

Your firm, controlled, and affectionate manner is good for this breed because it reacts strongly to stimulation. An over-stimulated Schnauzer is both hyper and noisy. Most of you run an orderly home, which is good discipline for a Schnauzer pup. The dog settles nicely in such a home. It will certainly protect all of the members of the household, but the pup often attaches particularly to one special person to whom it becomes devoted. This person is the one who feeds it, grooms it, trains it, and takes it for walks. Praise is important in training this one, along with doggie treats.

Because the dog is naturally protective, it will not accept strangers to your home right off the bat. It usually remains aloof until it decides whether the stranger is a threat to you. *Socialize* the pup at its special imprint time of three months by introducing it to as many friendly adults, children, and dogs as possible in pleasant surroundings. This will help the dog to be more calm and at ease when visitors come calling, but will not affect its excellent guarding abilities.

You'll have to brush this dog's coat regularly and give its beard and leg hair a trim. You can cut the dog's coat, but if you intend it for Show, a professional is advised. Stripping its coat is important, and this should be done about two or three times a year by a professional.

The Giant is usually too dignified to enjoy learning tricks and performing, but the Standard and the Miniature love to show off to an appreciative audience. If you let your Schnauzer know how special it is, it will strut with spirit and pride.

For exercise, the dog is willing to participate in whatever the family is up to – swimming, running, exploring trails, or playing fetch. It's an active dog that looks for fun days.

The next breed suggested for your personality, Virgo, is a breed with lots of connections.

KING CHARLES SPANIEL
Colors: Black and White
Height: 10"
Weight: 10 lbs.

This aristocratic little spaniel has been a member of court for centuries. Van Dyck painted several portraits of King Charles with his spaniels in the 17th century. The dog was known as the Toy Spaniel, but it became the King Charles due to its favor with the king.

Variations of the King Charles are the **PRINCE CHARLES**

(white with black and tan markings), the **RUBY** (chestnut red) and the **BLENHEIM** (white with red markings). A larger breed was developed in England from the Toy Spaniels and is known as the **CAVALIER KING CHARLES.** This spaniel can weigh up to 18 lbs., and is usually the color of the Ruby or the Blenheim.

The King Charles Spaniel is not temperamental. It's steady and level headed, full of affection for its owner once a bond has formed. It doesn't like to be rushed into new experiences, and likes to take its time. At first you will find your pup shy, but once it gains confidence, and gets used to the home and family, it fits in nicely. If you own a cat, the King Charles will probably seek it out for a best friend.

The dog enjoys the outdoors. It's a hardy breed, but if the dog gets wet, it's important to towel it dry and make sure its bed is dry and clean. You should bathe its face after an outing outdoors. The little dog is inquisitive, and could get grit in its eyes. Check with your vet about ear care.

Grooming is an easy chore for the dog's coat just needs to be brushed weekly, with little or no trimming required. Exercise is needed daily to keep the dog fit. It loves its food, and will turn its liquid eyes on anyone in the family that's eating something that smells good. Indulgent owners cause the dog to become obese, but you are not likely to do this.

Sweet, affectionate and playful, Toy Spaniels are very special and it's not surprising that they roamed palaces for centuries, beloved by kings, and have now become very popular pets, adored in countless homes.

Labrador Retrievers, Golden Retrievers, Gordon Setters, Norwegian Elkhounds, Airedales, Sealyhams, Schnauzers and King Charles Spaniels are the breeds we suggest for your sun sign personality, Virgo. We hope we have been of help to you.

Good luck in picking your perfect pup.

Labrador Retriever

Golden Retriever

Gordon Setter

Norwegian
Elkhound

Airedale Terrier

Sealyham
Terrier

Schnauzers

King Charles Spaniels

LIBRA THE SCALES
September 24 through October 23

Copper is your metal
Your stone is a sapphire
A forget-me-not is your flower
And your colors are pink, also pale blue
Now let's find that pup to help balance you

If you were taking a stroll through your neighborhood, and you saw two people walking their dogs greet each other as they passed, that's pleasant. If one of the dogs pulled free and lunged, snarling at the other, you would eye the aggressive dog with distaste. This is just not your kind of dog, Libra. But before we get into the breed traits and temperaments that would appeal to your personality, it's important to us that you know where we're coming from.

Initially, as a professional astrologer and a canine behaviorist, our first question was, "What kind of dog owner would a Libra be?". We found the answer by thoroughly studying your sun sign personality. Once we knew what you would probably look for in a dog, we considered all of the breeds registered with the American Kennel Club to find some perfect pups for you. Now, we're not saying that you can only successfully own the dogs we have selected for you. What we are saying is that the pups we suggest would be good choices for your sun sign personality.

We'll first review the characteristics of your sun sign, and discuss dog traits and temperaments that could be a plus or a minus for you. Your compatible pups are then described in full so that you can make your own decision based upon your lifestyle and personal preference.

Your sign shows you to be a person who seeks harmony and balance throughout your life. Harmony is almost as important to you as the air you breathe. In an atmosphere of discord and upset, you soon become plagued with the feeling of being unwell. If the situation continues, you feel positively ill. To flourish you need to be surrounded with peace and tranquility.

Many of you are very social people, and when you are on top form, you can be both articulate and charming. That's a winning combination. You can put smiles back on a face creased with frowns. When in a group, if you see a dispute about to erupt, you intervene with the skills of a diplomat. In fact,

Libra, you are a peacemaker.

Although you are often successful in restoring other people's calm, you can stir up quite a storm in personal situations where your own emotions are involved. In an argument, what is clear and reasonable to you is not always seen that way to others. When you can't get your point across, many of you become frustrated, and lose that Libran cool of yours completely. Your words can then become weapons. Only when you are calmer, can you give your opponent's arguements merit

Most of you strive to be fair. It's important to you to know all sides of an issue before you take a side. Whenever possible, you harvest all known information before you separate the grain from the chaff, and you are usually just in your conclusions. This is why some of you make excellent judges. On the other hand, because you need to see issues with high-definition clarity, you have a problem making decisions. If you are asked for a quick decision, your mind balks. How can you make an important decision when you don't know all of the facts? You certainly need time to think about it. Sometimes opportunities spring up, and are lost while you are still considering them. Some of you are left on the dock when the boat sails, trying to make up your mind whether or not to board.

At times, you have an abundance of energy, stimulated by interesting and creative careers or hobbies. You'll work lots of overtime, host a couple of parties, and run a dozen errands all in the same week. Such a busy pace will get to you, though, and you'll look for a chance to shut down for a while.

Many of you may be living a faster-paced life than truly suits you. When you feel the pressure of too many demands, you'll usually call a halt yourself, or a physical ailment will crop up to slow you down. You all have your own ways to unwind and look to yourselves. Some of you dim the lights, and turn on the music. Others may shop, read a novel, or watch a movie. You won't want to be bothered by anything or anyone at those times. It's time for you to refresh so that you can get back into the mainstream.

A variety of things interest you, Libra, and most of you have an insatiable curiosity. Some of you will explore different philosophies; the gossip column will fascinate others. What has been said, and by whom, is stimulating to your thought processes.

In keeping with your love of beauty and harmony, most you live in a home where the colors blend. Even if your home has only one or two rooms, it will probably be decorated in good taste and with some style. Wherever you live, you prefer to share your home with someone. Most of you dislike living alone.

You need a partner about to feel whole. You are not usually happy unless you can share your thoughts, ideas and plans with another. Talking about your life enhances it for most of you. Going it alone would not be a choice you would make voluntarily.

Your dog is certainly not likely to be the partner you seek, Libra, but the right kind of dog can ease the loneliness when relationships are just not working out.

As a dog owner you will be tolerant, and give your pup every chance to settle into the way you do things. Most of you will not be aggressive, harsh, or punitive in your handling of your dog, but you will expect it to do as it is told. You'll find no stimulation in arguments with a canine buddy, and most of you are not looking for a mega challenge in this area.

You'll probably read up on training your pup before you bring it home. Most of you will want to do your best to help the pup to understand what's expected of it. You'll be delighted with a pup that will learn with enjoyment, and remember what you have taught. Not all pups will do this to your satisfaction, though, so let's discuss the plus and minus breed traits and temperaments for your personality before we name the breeds suggested for you.

One of the things you don't need is an aggressive dog that loves to get into fights. They are immune to your charm, reason, and diplomacy, although some of you would try to talk sense into the dog. If you owned one, you would realize that the dog was over-protective out of its love for you, but that wouldn't change the unpleasant situations this dog could get you into. A dog that also enjoys a peaceful life would be more compatible with your personality.

Elegance pleases your eye. You will probably not be too keen on dogs with short legs, or stout dogs with wonderful ugly faces. Most of you look for beauty and style. Of course, if one of your canine friends is short, fat, and has a wonderful ugly face, you'll be the first the say what a devoted dog it is. If you are choosing the pup, though, you will probably seek a more graceful shape.

Shaggy dogs that attract mud, leaves, twigs, and fleas would make some of you shiver in horror. You'd have a problem letting one of these back into the house, unless it was a very stormy night. You'd also probably insist on giving it a bath before you allowed it to eat and sleep indoors. Now this could be the very night you had planned to be self-indulgent. That could be irritating. The dog gets to soak instead of you? Better to avoid the robust canines, even though some of them are super dogs.

A very demanding dog could get under your skin, Libra, and this could fester. You are perfectly willing to feed, groom, walk, and pet your dog, but enough is enough. When you want to take time for yourself, you shouldn't have to ask the dog's permission. A dog that will take "No" for its answer, and accept it, would be easier to live with for most of you.

To sum up, Libra, you don't need an aggressive dog that could make unpleasant scenes. Elegance and beauty is preferable to short and fat, robust mud magnets could offend your delicacy, and over-demanding dogs might upset your equilibrium.

As you consider the dogs suggested for you, remember your lifestyle. Although a dog may be right for your personality, it may not be right for where or how you live.

The first breed recommended for your personality is a lively, elegant pointer that may appeal to many of you.

HUNGARIAN VIZSLA
Colors: Dark yellow with red – golden rust
Height: 21"- 25"
Weight: 48 – 62 lbs.

The Viszla is extremely intelligent and sensitive, and when treated with respect, kindness, and affection it's an outstanding breed. Bred in Hungary, the Vizsla was the favored breed of barons and warlords of the Magyar tribes who settled in Hungary. Drawings of the Viszla date back to the 10th century.

This breed is intended to be an all-purpose dog. Trained in the right way, the dog excels at pointing, swimming, and retrieving. It's not difficult to train it to hunt, as it has a strong desire to please an owner it trusts. Although its coat is fine and short, it will perform well in all kinds of weather, and has no problems with any type of terrain.

This dog should not be housed outside. Its coat has no undercoat, and the dog has a strong need to be close to its owner. It's an excellent house-dog, clean in its habits, doesn't shed, and tunes in to its owner. Your pleasant style of training, combined with your expectation of obedience, would be good for this one. It's an affectionate dog, and will seek your company, but it's not intrusive or overly demanding.

Exercise is important. The country or the suburbs would be a better home than the city. Be sure to towel your dog dry after a romp in the rain, and it should have a bed of its own to curl up in on cold nights. Of course, the dog will attempt to climb under the covers with you. If you train the pup that lights out mean his own cozy bed, you'll have no problem.

Groom your Vizsla with a bristle brush. It will help the bonding between you in addition to keeping its coat clean and healthy. The dog doesn't have a doggy odor, even when wet, and a dry shampoo will freshen its coat.

As a pup, it's very playful, and quickly adores all members of the family. It's so happy to be with you all, though, it could knock down the toddlers.

Vizslas are highly strung when excited, untrained and young. *Socialize* your pup at its special imprint time of three months with as many adults, children, and other dogs as you can in pleasant surroundings. This will help to calm your dog when visitors are about.

The dog will respond to your personality, Libra. It should never be harshly trained. It wants to please you, and will do its best to do so. Believe it or not, this is a dog you can actually reason with. It will listen attentively when you have something to say, and try its best to understand. Needless to say, it will love the sound of your voice.

Remember the Vizsla is a larger breed, and moves out of its puppy stages slowly.

When you train your handsome pup with firmness, and praise, the dog will soon earn both your love and respect.

If you want to show your dog, you'll own a breed that has taken Best in Show, and is gaining in popularity on both sides of the Atlantic.

The next breed that may interest some of you is both graceful and beautiful.

SALUKI

Colors: Cream, fawn, white, black, amber, or combination
Height: 23"- 28"
Weight: 32 - 65 lbs.

Some authorities believe that this ancient Arabic hound comes from the town of Saluk in Southern Arabia, and the word 'saluki' means running hound in Arabic. It has been called the Persian Greyhound, also the Gazelle Hound. It's claimed that this dog runs faster than a Greyhound, but this is hard to prove since Salukis choose not to compete.

In Egyptian cultures the dogs were so esteemed that they were mummified with the bodies of their Pharaohs so they could travel with them on their journey to the afterlife. In Moslem cultures, where dogs are considered to be unclean, the Saluki is the exception. It is considered to have been blessed by Allah. This breed continues to be held in high regard in the Middle East.

Salukis were first brought to England in 1840, and eventually to the U.S. The AKC recognized the breed in 1927.

The Southern Illinois University sports teams have a Saluki for their mascot. The Southwest Tennessee Community College in Memphis, and Red Hill High School in Bridgeport, Illinois also favor the Saluki. One of the Amtrak trains serving Illinois is called the Saluki – probably a first time a train has been named after a dog, but we could be wrong.

In art, Saluki drawings were found on Egyptian tombs dating back to 2100 BC. They are portrayed in many paintings dating back centuries, and the 1951 Alberto Giacometti's sculpture entitled "Dog" is a Saluki.

Some of you will be enchanted with the special qualities of this lovable companion. It's a sweet, gentle, docile dog, affectionate to its owner, and to all family members. It always exhibits perfect manners, and is not only clean in its habits, it carries no doggy odor.

Your general pleasant manner will be good for this pup, which will not mature until well into its second year. Harsh treatment or punitive training would totally confuse a Saluki, and make it timid. Not only is it an intelligent breed, it wants to please. When your Saluki has made a mistake, it will be more upset than you are, and apologize in a fawning manner. It's extremely sensitive to your displeasure.

Sensitive in temperament does not mean it's a fragile breed. They may appear delicate, but Salukis are quite hardy. They love to romp and play, especially with other dogs. However, they dislike being muddy or dirty. If caught out in the rain, any self-respecting Saluki would appreciate a clean up and towel dry.

There are two varieties of this breed – those with soft, silky fringes on their ears and tails, and the totally smooth Saluki. Groom your Saluki with a hound glove to keep its coat soft and shiny. This is a great way to bond with your pup, and only groom when you are in a good mood, and feel affection for the dog. It will have radar where you are concerned.

Walking your Saluki will be a pleasant experience, but we wouldn't advise ever letting it off the leash. This is a pity because seeing your beautiful Saluki run with speed, grace and style would be uplifting for your spirit. The dog was born to hunt, though, and it could take off enthusiastically to seek a gazelle to chase. Since it's not likely to find one, it could decide to chase other prey, and you'd have a terrible time trying to catch your dog. It has been clocked at over 40 mph.

If you live in the country and have land, be sure your fence is at least six feet high, Sulukis can jump fences. Check that the fences are sound, otherwise you could have angry farmers come calling. If you have other pets, vigilance would also be advised. This dog wouldn't understand why it couldn't chase them, and would do so on impulse when they ran.

If the dog is leashed when out, and not allowed to roam free, it's a perfectly well-behaved dog.

Salukis do not bark a lot. They make their hound sound, which to some is musical. Making a fuss about nothing is not this hound's style, though, and it will only warn you when intruders are about.

Like you, Libra, the dog needs private time to curl up and relax. It will disappear in your home from time to time to do this, but most of you will understand this all too well. You might have to remind the children that the dog shouldn't be bothered when it wants to be alone.

The city or the suburbs are fine for this breed if you walk your dog often.

Your vet will be cautious, we're sure, but due to the Saluki's lack of body fat, anesthetics must be used carefully.

A Saluki is certainly a refined pet, and here's another one with excellent manners and a loving heart.

WHIPPET
Colors: Black, red, white, fawn or blue, also mixed coloring.
Height: 19"- 22"
Weight: 25 – 45 lbs.

The Whippet is a sweetheart. It's a gentle dog, Libra, just right for those of you who are looking for a constant companion. The dog has charming manners, both in the home and outside, and will look to you for approval and love for all of its life.

The breed was developed in England. Whippet racing was a very popular sport in the 19th century. Whippets were also bred for hunting game by sight. They coursed game at high speeds. It was the English mill operators who brought the dog to the U.S. and the AKC recognized it in 1888.

Greyhounds, Italian Greyhounds, Manchester Terriers, Airedales, and English terriers are said to be in the mix, but authorities differ. They also differ on why the Whippet is known as the snap-dog. One authority claims that when dogs met on a straight course, they snapped at each other. Another claims that it is because the dog can change its direction without slowing down. Without a doubt, this dog is as quick as a whip.

It's an easy dog to keep clean, Libra. Its coat is short, soft and silky to the touch, and its little feet leaves small prints. Groom your dog to calm it, and to keep its coat shiny and clean. It's a good idea to rub the dog down with a piece of chamois leather.

The dog is very quiet in the home, but when outside, make sure you have a fenced yard. This dog can be gone in a matter of seconds if a rabbit happens by. The dog is usually good at playing catch, and at agility games. If you live in the city, in an apartment, that's fine so long as you walk the dog. If you have interest in seeing the dog run, you can do so by entering the dog in Whippet races, or lure coursing. Whippets also show well.

Socialize this sweet pup when its three months old by introducing it to as many friendly adults, children, and dogs as possible in pleasant surroundings. This will help to calm the dog when strangers are about, but it is not a watchdog, and is usually friendly to visitors unless they are loud and boisterous people.

It's easy to train. You won't even have to raise your voice, but it's important to remember that Whippets grow out of their puppy stages slowly, and are not mature until well into their second year. Pushing a Whippet is not wise. The dog is usually submissive to its owner. Anyone who shouts a lot at a Whippet will have trouble finding the dog. It will hide away. Since most of you avoid violence in any form, and prefer a peaceful home, a Whippet should be happy with you.

This gentle dog is often used as a therapy dog for the aged and infirm.

If you live where winters are cold, you'll need a coat for your dog, and it should always be housed inside. As your vet will advise, careful use of anesthesia is important, and some Whippets have an irregular heart beat when at rest. This is said to be common for a Whippet, and the dog has a regular heartbeat when exercised.

The dogs we have suggested so far have fine coats, but perhaps you are looking for an attractive dog with a beautiful furry coat.

SHETLAND SHEEPDOG (SHELTIE)
Colors: Tricolor, sable or white, blue
Height: 13"-16"
Weight: 14 - 16lbs.

Once a Sheltie has attached, it becomes a part of its owner. The dog is so highly attuned to its owner's whereabouts, it actually senses when he or she is close to home, and is at the door long before the key turns in the lock.

The breed is Scottish. It's thought that the Border Collie is in its mix. The English Kennel Club recognized the breed in 1909, and the first Sheltie, Lord Scott, was registered with the AKC in 1914.

It's a three-purpose breed – an affectionate pet, fine show dog, and an alert watchdog. Actually, it's quite a good baby sitter, too. Shelties often follow their young charges about to herd them from harm.

A Sheltie will not accept your visitors easily. The dog is usually reserved with strangers. If you entertain a lot, introduce your pup to friendly people and other canines at its special imprint time of about twelve weeks. *Socializing* the dog will help it to be less suspicious of friends dropping by, but will not affect its protective instincts. It takes its job as watchdog very seriously.

Undue harshness will quickly destroy a Sheltie's trust. Aggressive and punitive treatment would drastically change this dog's natural sweet behavior. Your easy style of training, with expectations of good behavior is good for this breed. Intense training is not necessary. The dog is intelligent and extremely eager to please. Your firm voice will quickly bring the dog to obedience.

A Sheltie will not invade your space, but it does like to keep you in its sight at all times. When it takes a nap, it is more contented if this could be inches from your feet.

Outside, the dog is very lively, and likes to play. You'll find it behaves well on long walks. On your return, your Sheltie will probably clean its own paws

Brush your Sheltie's coat once a week, to keep it looking smart, and if you intend to show your dog, a professional is advised. You might want to enter the dog in Obedience. It has done well here.

Hot climates are really not good for a Sheltie as the dog was bred to withstand the harsh windy, wet weather of the Scottish moors. It's a good dog for the city, country or the suburbs, though.

The next breed we suggest for you, Libra, is sure to win many of you over totally.

BOXER
Colors: Fawn or brindle with white markings
Height: 21"- 25"
Weight: 55 – 70 lbs

The Boxer is a beautiful dog, Libra. It bounds when it walks, sits erect, and looks quite noble as it surveys its world.

The Boxer we know today started in Munich, Germany in 1896. Opinions vary but it's thought to be descended from the Tibetan Mastiff, with some Bulldog and possibly Great Dane in its mix. The breed was first registered in America in 1904. The breed's climb to popularity was slow at first until people learned the dog had a very sweet nature, and Boxers took the honors at shows.

Although the Boxer is a large dog, it's happy in an apartment, town house, country mansion, cottage, or suburban home. When trained, it's extremely well behaved. You'll respond to its affectionate nature, and its keen interest in whatever you may be doing or saying. In fact, Boxers love to communicate as much as you do, Libra, and are intuitively wise to their owner's moods.

Because these dogs are responsible in the home, intelligent, and easily trained, they have become favored guide dogs for the blind. They are also K-9 recruits for the police and army. Boxers are known for being able to serve in whatever capacity required of them. They have an even temperament along with an inquisitive nature, keen mind and social graces.

Although your Boxer enjoys hanging out with friendly people, when you leave it at home alone it will play happily for hours with its toys. Of course, you may find that old teddy bear you saved from childhood missing. Check your dog's bed. You'll probably find it stashed next to the green squeaky frog, rubber ball, one of your socks, and a rawhide strip.

If you have children, your Boxer will love them. Kids are wonderful playmates for a dog that, even when old and gray, always wants to play. *If you have cats, though, don't get a Boxer.* Some Boxers find a cat chase impossible to resist, delight in treeing felines, and will spend hours tracking them down in the home.

If you live where the winters are cold, you'll have to go shopping for sweaters for this one. Its coat is very fine and soft, and doesn't keep out the chill winds. Save your old towels, too. When your Boxer has been out in the rain, you should dry it off. If you live where the summers are hot, air conditioning is a must. Boxers shiver in the cold and pant in the heat.

Is it a guard dog? Opinions differ on this question, and it's possible that the dog behaves according to whether it feels an intruder intends bodily harm. Samantha–*see front cover*– alerts her owner to all passers by with low growls and barks. She is definitely a good watchdog.

Most Boxers do not respond well to total strangers, and are wary of them. *Socialize* your Boxer pup by taking it out to meet and greet people, and other dogs, at its special imprint time of three months. It would also be a good idea, Libra, if you did not get the pup when you plan to be away a lot. Your Boxer will choose its favorite person as a pup, so make sure you are a constant with your pup during its imprint time.

When people have had a Boxer as a member of the family, they rarely want any other breed. It's just that kind of dog.

However, some of you may be looking for a spaniel breed, and if so, this one should win your heart.

BRITTANY SPANIEL
Colors: White with red or orange patches
Height: 18" - 20"
Weight: 30 - 40 lbs.

You may come across this breed in black and white, and liver and white, but red or orange and white is usually favored with the dog's eyes, dark amber, and its nose, pinky-brown. Its coat is very soft and silky with light feathering on its throat, stomach and legs. The Brittany Spaniel is a very attractive dog.

It's possible that the French and the Welsh came up with the dog that we know today, as Welsh Springer Spaniels are similar to the Brittany. The breed was not registered with the American Kennel Club until 1934.

This dog is gentle, eager to please, and is highly intelligent. *If, however, the pup is punished harshly it will not grow into its potential.* Most of you wouldn't think of treating your puppy harshly, though, so the pup should be safe with you.

If you hunt, or are interested in Field Trials, you'll find that the Brittany has a dual personality. It's courageous and tough in the field, but gentle and devoted as a pet. Speed at the hunt is the Brittany's style. It's very quick, agile, and has no fear of brambles. At times, it does lose its concentration when affected by other stimuli, but if you give your dog a firm, but friendly reminder to stay on task, your Brittany will excel. The breed has done well at the American National Field trials.

Like most spaniels, this dog is sensitive, Libra, so don't forget to introduce your Brittany pup to friends, strangers, and other dogs at its critical imprint time of twelve weeks. It'll help the dog to feel more comfortable at social gatherings for all of its life. Everyone will respond to this sweet, soft, wriggly bundle of charm.

Introduce your pup to water in a fun and easy-going way, also, so you can have fun with your Brittany at the lake or at the ocean.

If you live in the country or in the suburbs, you'll have a happier spaniel. The dog loves to go for a walk, and to be able to use its excellent nose in the woods and trails. Be sure you have trained your pup before you unclip its leash, though. It could scent something fascinating and take off with incredible speed.

The dog's coat will need regular brushing and trimming from time to time. You should start early, taking over where the pup's mother left off. Grooming your spaniel will cement the bonding process, and you will love how fine your dog looks after grooming.

Spaniels often have ear problems, but this is easily prevented. Check with your vet about ear care.

The Brittany is a good sporting dog. Perhaps, though, some of you are looking for a terrier breed, liking the inquisitive, sweet nature so true of most terriers. If so, this one is very popular.

WEST HIGHLAND WHITE TERRIER
Color: White
Height: 10"- 11"
Weight: 15 - 18 lbs.

This little dog will put a grin on your face most of the time, Libra.

The Westie is fun. Not only is it an outgoing little dog, it's bright, loves to play, is a good watchdog, and very affectionate.

Originally bred to flush badgers and foxes from hiding places in the rocky terrains of Scotland, the Westie came in all colors. However, multi-colored dogs were sometimes mistaken for the game they flushed. They were then bred to be all white for their own safety. The breed was once known by many other names, too, Pittenweems, Poltallochs, and Roseneaths - named for the areas in which they lived. In the early 1900's the name West Highland White became official.

The Westie made its debut in show business at *Crufts* in London, England in 1907. Nowadays, it's a breed to contend with competitively. It seems to enjoy being on center stage at Show, and is a pert, happy participant, usually delighted to meet the judges.

Your Westie will quickly learn what you expect from it, and will be eager to please you. However, determination, along with an inquisitive nature is part of the Westie's charm. You'll have to be firm at times without being too harsh or punitive.

A regular brush and trim keeps this little dog looking smart. It has a double, thick coat that enables it to handle all weathers. If you decide to take your dog along, most Westies travel well. When the dog stays home alone, it will take its job as watchdog quite seriously, and give you an enthusiastic welcome when you return. If you plan on being away for a long time, your Westie will probably get restless. Some Westie owners buy a pair if their lifestyles include long absences from home. If you are a part of a family, though, or live with friends, your Westie will miss you, but will be contented with them. It's a sociable little dog.

If any of you are looking for a Toy, here are two that might interest you. One has curly hair, the other is sleek and silky.

BICHON FRISE
Colors: White, White with shades of cream, apricot or gray
Height: No more than 12"
Weight: 7 - 12 lbs.

For a little dog, this breed has quite a history. The dog is descended from the Barbet or water spaniel, and the Poodle. The Mediterranean area was its home. Bichons were popular with sailors, and were their companions on their ships, which sailed from continent to continent. Spanish seamen brought the breed to the Canary Island of Tenerife, and in the 1300s, Italian sailors took the little dogs on their voyages. They were favored by Italian nobility, and then taken up by street vendors.

The Bichon Frise was highly favored by the kings and queens of

France, and painted by the masters. In the late 19th century it became highly popular both as a pet and a circus performer all over Europe. In 1956 Americans were introduced to the Bichon Frise, but it was not until 1972 that the AKC declared the breed pure and eligible for show.

You will recognize a strong need in this one, Libra. It loves to be part of a happy and loving group of people, and is at its best as part of a family. The Bichon has a merry spirit, and does well in a harmonious household.

If you live alone, and travel often, a Bichon is not a good choice for you. The dog becomes uneasy when left on its own for long periods. However, if you live in a family, a Bichon will not pine as it becomes fond of all of its people.

Because its coat does not shed, it can matt. You'll need to bathe and groom this pup on a regular basis. For Show, a professional is advised.

A Bichon is intelligent, and will delight you with what it manages to learn all by itself. Because it will be attentive to your wishes, you should have no problems with training this one. Certainly, the little dog is high-spirited, and, as a pup, will probably get into lots of mischief, but a Bichon Frise will put more grins on your face than frowns. It's such a merry companion.

The next Toy breed is a dog with a different type of temperament.

ITALIAN GREYHOUND
Colors: Various
Height: 13"- 15"
Weight: No more than 11lbs.

This dog is an ancient breed, going back for centuries. In the middle ages, the dog was seen all over Southern Europe, and was favored by Italians. It's because of its popularity with Italians that it became known as the Italian Greyhound. Several of the great masters painted the dog, and the breed has been a favorite of Kings and Queens. During the reign of Queen Victoria, the dog was very popular in England, as the Queen adored her little dogs.

The first Italian Greyhound was registered with the AKC in 1886.

The dog is a one-person dog, Libra. Quite early on, the dog will attach to you, and you will become the sun, the moon, and the stars all rolled into one. Other people are usually treated with reserve.

Usually when one sees a sign "Beware of the Dog" it means a guard dog is on the premises, but signs were posted for the Italian Greyhound meaning that people should be careful with the dog. It has a fine bone structure, and it would not be difficult to break its leg if a gate was shoved open.

This dog is only for Libras willing to nurture the dog. Its coat is very short and silky, and it feels the cold. The dog will need its bed and blankets to snuggle into. On walks, if its chilly, you'd need to put a warm sweater on your little friend, and have a spare in the closet for rainy days.

It's a picky eater in that it eats when it feels like it, and not necessarily on a regular basis. Exercise helps to keep its appetite good, and it's important to walk the dog to keep its muscle tone in good order. Unfortunately it has a small bladder, and needs understanding when it comes to training the dog in this area. It can be trained, of course, but needs more time than some breeds. If you live where it's cold and windy, you could put some newspaper by the front or back door, as the dog will be reluctant to go out in that kind of weather.

Pampering your Italian Greyhound in its care is one thing, but you should not over protect the dog. It has a finely tuned, and adventurous spirit, which could be destroyed by too much babying as much as by harsh treatment. Its size and delicate appearance could turn any owner into an anxious parent, but that's why we suggest it for you, Libra. If allowed to develop naturally, the dog will delight you with its intelligence and lively nature. An Italian Greyhound should not be seen shivering and quivering on a lap, but prancing happily besides its owner, full of life and energy.

The Hungarian Viszla, Whippet, Shetland Sheepdog, Boxer, Brittany Spaniel, West Highland White, Bichon Frise and the Italian Greyhound are the breeds we suggest for your sun sign personality, Libra. We hope we have been of help to you.

Good luck in picking your perfect pup.

Hungarian Viszla

Whippet

Sheltie

Boxer

Brittany Spaniel

West
Highland
White

Bichon Frise

Italian Greyhound

SCORPIO THE SCORPION
SCORPIO THE EAGLE
October 24 through November 22

Plutonium is your metal
Your stone is an opal
Rhododendron is your plant
And your color is wine
Now let's seek that special canine

If you were visiting relatives who owned a dog, you would be interested in getting to know their pet. However, if the dog couldn't be still for a moment or two, and dashed about doing four different things in about the same amount of minutes, you would quickly lose interest. Lightweights are not your kind of dog. But before we discuss the breed traits and temperaments that would appeal to your Scorpio personality, it's important to us that you understand where we're coming from.

Initially, as a professional astrologer and a canine behaviorist, our first question was, "What kind of dog owner would a Scorpio be?". We found the answer by thoroughly studying your sun sign personality. Once we knew what you would probably look for in a dog, we considered all of the breeds registered with the American Kennel Club to find some perfect pups for you. Now, we're not saying that you can only successfully own the dogs we have selected for you. What we are saying is that the pups we suggest would be good choices for your sun sign personality.

We'll first review the characteristics of your sun sign, and discuss dog traits and temperaments that could be a plus or a minus for you. Your compatible pups are then described in full so that you can make your own decision based upon your lifestyle and personal preference.

Your sign shows you to be a person with an intense emotional personality, but this is not obvious to the casual observer. On the surface many of you are quiet, laidback people. This is as misleading as you intend it to be. You control your feelings most of the time, and usually present yourself to the world in general as cool, calm and collected.

Your body language may be casual, Scorpio, but your eyes usually give you away. When you feel a spark of interest in someone or something, your gaze is penetrating.

Most of you do not want to waste your time on what you feel is trivia. Cocktail chatter becomes tiring for you within minutes; lightweight people and casual conversations hold little interest for you. Although you may enjoy parties occasionally as an observer, you usually prefer your conversations to be one-on-one, and serious in content.

Some of you are good listeners. You are genuinely interested in people's secrets and problems, and have a natural ability to probe. In fact, you can ferret out more information than the person intended to share. You may give general sympathy, even empathy, but it's not likely that you will share your secrets in return. You are usually extremely private people.

Mediocrity in all things will bore you. Most of you are not only intelligent, but inwardly seek the power to utilize your abilities to the full. If you find your niche, you become dedicated to your job. A strong will, along with an ability to pursue your goal relentlessly, makes you a force to be reckoned with.

Life is a serious affair to most of you. Pluto, the planet of power and intensity is your ruler. Your inner reactions are usually extreme. When angry, your fury is volcanic, and when happy, you are ecstatic. You take no incident that affects your emotions lightly.

If you have chosen a really worthy cause to be your life's work, it will bring out the best in you. Most of you will be able to make a complete commitment to it.

You spend your lives looking for that which is of true worth. If you can find a passion to focus upon, you will soar like an eagle. If your quest is unfulfilled, you will feel the sting of the scorpion.

No dog could possibly qualify for your inner search, Scorpio, but life is filled with many outlets. Your dog can certainly be one of these. Some of you will be quite special dog owners. Unless you have had a good relationship with a dog in the past, it's doubtful that you have a specific breed in mind. Some of you will hug a pup and just know it's the right one for you. We'll go into the minus and plus breed traits and temperaments for your general personality now to give you an idea of which breed pups you should check out with your intuitive hugs. Actually, some of you are capable of such compassion, you could end up with the wrong dog for all the right reasons.

What would be the perfect pup for a Scorpio personality? Certainly, it should not be a lightweight. A dog with a short attention span that dashes hither and thither chasing butterflies would amuse you for five minutes, and then be dismissed. Many of you will choose your dog's company over other people's at times, and would be much more interested in a breed that is not only intelligent, but also capable of concentrated determination. This could be its job of protecting you, hunting with you, going for Best in Show, or just giving you the kind of loyalty and devotion you respect.

Talkative canines without purpose in their endless barking could light your fuse. You would become thoroughly irritated being around such breeds. A fuss about nothing would irritate most of you.

To be fair to those excited canines, they truly wouldn't deserve your power packed advance if they refused to settle down at your first or second command to do so. They may need to communicate something to you - something they think you should know. Perhaps there's a cheeky squirrel running up and down your fence, or visitors are talking to your neighbors out in front, and they have stepped on your lawn, twice. Maybe the mail carrier came, and rattled your box again! It could be that those trash collectors drove up and stole all your terrific-smelling garbage, even though they've been warned every week not to do that any more. You may not realize just how important all this stuff is to some canines.

Since most of you have no idea how strong your controlled anger is, you might be quite perplexed as to why the excited, talkative dog suddenly freezes into a crouched position, quivering, before you get within five feet of it. And if it doesn't react that way, it could take off at your approach like a scared rabbit. If your dog did that, it will have really blown it. You'll be furious. There will be little control in your reactions at this turn of events, and the dog will probably keep on heading that a way.

Of course, none of this is fated to happen, Scorpio. You can choose a pup that does not stir up your inner emotions in a negative way – a dog that will hush-up when you command it to do so, if not the first time, certainly the second.

Ever heard the common saying, "Our dog owns us, we don't own our dog"? Well, it's doubtful that most of you would say this. There are some breeds, though, independent enough to attempt a take over bid, and keep trying, immune even to Scorpio wrath. These dogs do their own thing. In part, you might admire their spirit, and even respect their courage, but a dog that recognizes your superiority, and flourishes because of it, is more the dog for you.

Most of you are incredibly loyal in your personal commitments once such a commitment is made. You will expect your dog to have this quality. Your dog does not have to love the world and its people. You certainly don't. It does have to love you unreservedly if it is to win your love in return.

To sum up then, Scorpio, the perfect pup for your personality must not be a lightweight. It must be intelligent and dedicated. Noisy dogs and fidgets would get under your skin, and independent dogs would not give you the respect you would demand from your dog. Finally, and most importantly, your dog should be loyal and faithful.

As you explore all of the breeds suggested for you Scorpio, please remember that your lifestyle is as important as that intuitive link you could make with your perfect pup.

The first breed discussed for your interest will appeal to some of you. It's truly exceptional.

DOBERMAN PINSCHER
Colors: Black, brown, gray-blue with rust markings.
Height: 24"- 28"
Weight: 65 - 90 lbs.

The Doberman is one of the most intelligent, loyal, protective breeds known to man. Most of you will particularly appreciate this dog's ability to understand what is required, and its single-minded devotion to the task. This dog thinks, reasons, solves problems, and is dedicated to serving its owner in every way possible. It excels at guard work, as a protective companion, and if socialized, does well as a show dog.

Herr Louis Dobermann spent over twenty years perfecting this breed in Germany. He was a tax collector who traveled a lot in his work. He needed a loyal, protective dog and set about to breed his ideal traveling companion. What went into a Dobe was kept a secret, but it is thought that Thuringian Shepherds, Black and Tan Terriers, Beaucerons and Greyhounds may have contributed to the breed. Another authority suggests that there was some German Pinscher in the mix, and yet another suggests a Rottweiler. Well, like many of your secrets, Scorpio, a Dobe's true ingredients will probably remain a mystery only to be guessed at.

A Doberman instinctively knows that it is a dog of great distinction. The dog has the natural air of pride and confidence of a dominant breed. It needs a superior strength to its own to lead its pack. This dog needs direction, and must be under its owner's control at all times. Your inner strength is good for this one. The dog is intuitive and sensitive enough to sense your disapproval before a power packed advance would be necessary. The dog will not only watch and listen, it will learn.

As with all of the larger breeds, puppy stages move slowly. Your Dobe pup will not be a mature dog until well into its second year. You would be wise to take this into account when you're evaluating the dog's performance. It may look grown up at six months, but it's still a tender, eager pup inside that strong muscular body. It will need many more months to truly reach its superb potential.

Guarding you comes naturally to a Dobe. How suspicious the dog is depends upon you. It's important to take your pup where it can meet strangers, adults and children, with their dogs, in pleasant circumstances at its special imprint time of about three months. Although we know it's not something you would choose to do normally, it is important to *socialize* your Doberman pup. It will make the dog steadier and less suspicious for the rest of its life. It will still be aloof to strangers until you welcome them to your home, and although it will not be aggressive towards them, it will keep an eye on them during their visit.

Dobermans are often used as guard dogs for stores and other commercial houses. The police are always on the look out for fine examples of this breed to recruit, as are the military. The breed has distinguished itself in war. In fact, there is a life-size bronze statue of a Doberman, *Always Faithful* at Guam's War Dog cemetery at the U.S. Naval Base in Orote Point.

The dog needs exercise. If you have a backyard, it must be fenced. Of course, it will enjoy talking long walks with you. Although some people house this dog outside, we recommend that the dog live in your home. It's a clean dog, with minimal grooming requirements, and it has a need to be near, and to protect its primary person. When you give your dog a rub down with a rubber glove mitt, you will be exercising your right as Alpha – the leader of its pack – and will help to increase the bonding between you.

Caging the dog is not a good idea, but this doesn't include crating the pup to keep it safe in early training. The dog should also not be chained up.

In the U.S. many Dobermans have cropped ears. In England, they do not. You can discuss cropping the ears of your Doberman pup with your vet. If you intend to show the dog in the U.S., it's advisable. If not, it's a matter of personal preference.

We should warn you, Scorpio, that you must do a good background check on bloodlines before you get your pup from a reputable breeder. A true Doberman is a treasure. Unfortunately there are breeders who have tried to "improve" on the dog. Some Dobermans are too highly strung, and are therefore unpredictable; others have been bred to be attack dogs, and are too aggressive. You can still get a true Doberman pup if you spend some time to investigate breeders.

For those of you looking for a serious, but rewarding challenge in dog owning, a Doberman will be a good choice, but if you are looking for a ball of fur that will grow into a strong dog, check out this one.

AKITA
Colors: Any color, brindle or pinto
Height: 24"- 28"
Weight: 75 - 88lbs.

The Akita is a respected member of many families in Japan, admired for its boldness, courage, intelligence and versatility. It's also known as a Large or Shishi Inu. A nobleman, who lived in the Akita Province in the early 1600's, is credited with the breed. At that time, only a noble family could adopt an Akita, and the dog represented good health and fortune for the family. When a baby is born, an Akita statue is presented to the child to bring the child luck – happiness and a long life.

Helen Keller was presented with an Akita in 1937, but the breed was not really known in the U.S. until post World War II when servicemen brought the dog home with them.

Most of you look for substance before making a commitment, and this dog is exceptional. It has tremendous courage, and is dedicated to serving its owner in whatever capacity asked of it. It's not likely that any of you will ask your Akita to slay a wild boar for you, dragons being a touch hard to find even in Japan, but this dog wouldn't hesitate to take one on.

The Akita has been called aloof. It often is with strangers. However, being aloof with strangers would not be considered to be a fault for most of you. You would probably see it as an attribute. Still, it's a good idea to *socialize* this sweet furry pup at about three months old, which is its special imprint time. Introduce the pup to friendly people, and other canines in pleasant circumstances. The dog will be less suspicious of your friends and relatives, will do better at Show, but will retain its reserve with total strangers.

It's not hard to train the Akita, but it does require an owner who has strength of purpose. If the dog senses you are a pushover, it could use this to its own advantage. It's not likely to sense this with most of you, though, Scorpio. A few have made that mistake to their cost. Once your Akita knows you are in charge, and understands your high expectations, it will settle to a lifetime of serving you with excellence.

Brushing your Akita's coat regularly will do more than groom your pup. It will help to cement the growing bond between you, and will let the pup know who is now in charge. Grooming was one of the ways its mother kept it in line. Feeding the pup, teaching it manners, and taking it for walks is all part of the bonding process. When the dog has attached through its respect for you, it should flourish in your care. You will form a mutual relationship of worth. For many of you, there is no other kind.

The breed has very keen eyesight, and was bred for the hunt. Off leash, the dog should be kept to your own property with a fence in place. Although the dog's coat will protect it in cold weather, it is advisable not to kennel the dog outside. Being a part of you and your home is important to an Akita to maintain its bonding and attachment.

An Akita's inner eyes are almost as sharp as their dark, outer ones. This dog has a sixth sense when it comes to its owner and handler, and will respond quickly to moods and situations.

The army recruits Akitas. They are very good guard dogs. The dog is incapable of betrayal, and is loyal. A charming story surfaced in researching this dog. A Japanese man who took a train to work every day owned an Akita named Hachiko. The dog met his owner's train every night. When the man died, Hachiko continued to meet his train until the day he died.

Dobermans and Akitas are both special canines in their own ways, but perhaps you are looking for a medium-sized terrier of substance. This one is special for the right owner.

BULL TERRIER
Color: White, white with brindle coloring
Height: 21"- 22"
Weight: 40 - 50lbs.

Perhaps what you will like most about this intelligent breed, Scorpio is that it's known for its intuitive sense. Bull Terriers actually anticipate their owners' needs, and the dog is uncanny in its ability to sense people who are up to no good.

Bull Terriers date back to the mid nineteenth century. A Bulldog was mated with the English White Terrier.

Just about everybody knows this breed as it has a famous history. It's the Target mascot, and Budweiser's Spuds McKenzie. Bull Terriers are very trainable, and not at all camera shy. The dog has appeared in many movies and T.V. series, too numerous to name. You may remember that in the movie *Oliver*, Bill Sykes dog was a Bull Terrier. The U.S. General, George S. Patton, owned a Bull Terrier named Willie – named after William the Conqueror.

Grooming is minimal, and it's a clean dog. If you live where there are a lot of mosquitoes and fleas, you should protect the dog as much as possible. Bull Terriers can be allergic to insect bites, and get a rash. They can also be born deaf, so be sure to check your pup out carefully when purchasing it.

You'll find this pup to be a ball of energy, Scorpio, so it'll be up to you not to let it over do, and damage its growing muscles and tendons. It loves to romp and play. When mature, the dog will need exercise and will love to go on long walks with you.

The breed shows well, and has taken home the coveted Best in Show in the U.S., in England, and also in South Africa and Australia. It has a jaunty, confident step in the ring, and definitely smiles at the judges.

Your pup will need your firm hand initially, as it is a breed that needs an Alpha – a leader for its pack. It's important, though, that you treat the dog with firmness and not aggressiveness. A harshly treated Bull Terrier pup will grow up to be an aggressive dog instead of the friendly, loyal, and obedient dog it's meant to be. Train with a positive, firm hand, and definitely use treats as rewards for lessons learned.

The dog is active and very friendly except at times with other dogs. In its history, its ancestors probably fought in the ring. *Socialize* the pup at the usual imprint time of twelve weeks with as many people and other dogs as you can to help the pup to be more relaxed when company visits with their dogs. Once the dog knows that friends are visiting, it will delight in their company, but should an intruder visit, you'll have an exceptional watchdog.

You will respond to this pup because once it has attached to you, it will love you with devotion and respect for all of its life. The dog listens, is able to process your commands, thinks, problem solves, and tries to please – definitely a winner for some of you.

A similar breed in intelligent traits and spirited temperament is the **STAFFORDSHIRE BULL TERRIER.** The unfortunate connection with this breed to Pit Bulls has done serious damage to this fine dog's reputation. Staffordshires have been part of the breed recipe for Pits, along with others. The purebred Staffordshire is excellent with older children (a tad too exuberant in its affection for tots), and is friendly with adults who intend no harm to the family.

Particularly if the pup is male, it may well grow up to be aggressive to other male dogs. Your strong control and respect for a dog of substance would be good for this breed. It's not a dog one adopts lightly. It needs guidance, and to be disciplined by a firm and affectionate hand. People with aggressive natures and short fuses do not bring out the best in this pup when one is looking for the finer qualities of a Staffordshire.

The next breed suggested for you, Scorpio, is not only a sporting breed, it's a wonderful family dog.

LABRADOR RETRIEVER
Colors: Black, chocolate, yellow
Height: 21"- 24"
Weight: 55 - 80lbs.

Of all the sporting breeds in the U.S., Labrador Retrievers are undoubtedly the most popular breed. It's truly an exceptional dog. As a pup, it strives to please, and should delight even the most demanding Scorpios. Highly intelligent, easily trained, and capable of great devotion, a Labrador Retriever definitely qualifies as one of mankind's best friends.

Originally Labs were bred on the island of Newfoundland, which is now a province of Newfoundland and Labrador, Canada. Some authorities claim that the dog was once named the St. John's dog, used to help the fisherman in the St. John's area of Newfoundland. Others say that the

Newfoundland was the St. John's dog, but the Labrador definitely has a Newfoundland in its mix. The British are credited with developing the breed we know today.

This dog's talents cover a broad range. The breed is used for hunting, tracking, retrieving, police work, search and rescue, guide dogs, aids for the disabled, agility and obedience. It would be impossible to name all the famous Labradors, but most of you would enjoy hearing about some of them. Jake is a national canine hero, searching and rescuing survivors of 9/11. He was also called into service for Hurricane Katrina victims. Lucky and Flo, are counterfeit dogs, and sniffed out nearly 2 million pirated counterfeit DVD's. Buddy and Seamus are good friends of former President, Bill Clinton, and Russian President Vladimir Putin's has a Lab named Koni. Endal, a British Lab, is the most photographed Lab. Among other things, Endal was the first dog to ride on the London Eye, and the first dog known to work an ATM. Reportedly, they are making a film about Endal's exploits into fame. Rascal was the first chocolate Lab to win the National Field Trial Championship and you probably know Bouncer in *Neighbors*, and Luath in *The Incredible Journey*. The Memphis Mad Dogs have a Lab as their mascot.

If you are looking for a hunting dog, Scorpio, this one is tireless in the field, and excellent in water. It ignores bad weather conditions, and has an obvious love of the sport. If you do not hunt, your dog might do some hunting on its own. Our black Lab, Hector, often brought us a live pheasant or a duck when we were out walking in the fields. Carried in his soft mouth, the birds were complaining, but unharmed. The same dog could also be counted on to bring us the children's escaped guinea pigs and hamsters that only he could find, and they were always unharmed when he dropped them into the children's laps.

Retrieving something, anything, and bringing it to you is often the way this dog shows its love for you. When you come home, your Lab will probably bring you a present. Now this could be anything within its reach, maybe a shoe, a hat, glove or a sock, and it will be presented to you with barely-contained joy. This is its natural behavior and come from when hunters praised their dogs for retrieving downed birds. A retriever should not be scolded for being itself. If you'd like to keep your shoes, gloves or socks in pairs, keep a couple of the dog's toys by the front and back doors. Your dog will present those to you quite happily as your welcome-home gift.

The bond between you will grow quickly, and the pup will scamper after you from room to room. The pup needs to attach, and it will develop well with an affectionate and companionable owner. Left too much on its own, without human companionship, it could become depressed, and then positively mournful if things do not improve.

Children and Labs get along very well, and the dog likes most adults. They can be quite choosy about being friends with just any dog, though, and can be aggressive to visiting canines. *Socialize* your pup at its special imprint time of three months with as many friendly adults, children, and other dogs as you can in pleasant surroundings. This will help the dog to be less suspicious of strangers to your home, but will not affect its watchdog traits.

Because Labrador Retrievers are intuitive to their owner's needs and super-protective, your dog will watch you, and assess your mood, Scorpio. Your firmness, along with your affection, is needed to keep this lovable dog under control. Training with physical punishment is not necessary. The tone of your voice works wonders with this one. Labs are proud to please you. When the pup does well, be sure to give it a dog treat along with your praise.

Exercise is important, and your yard should be fenced. Grooming its coat is not difficult – a brush with a good bristle brush should do it, but if you live by the ocean, and the dog is constantly in the water, wash off the salty water at the end of the day to avoid dermatitis.

If you remember that puppy stages last longer in larger breeds, a Lab can be everything you want in a dog. It will turn inside out to please you and rarely, if ever, let you down.

In our opinion, the color of the pup is important. Black Labs are mellower - Chocolate Labs are more highly strung, and impulsive at times - Yellow Labs are more independent. Certainly they are all beautiful dogs, Scorpio, but a Black or Yellow might be more what you are looking for.

The next breed we suggest was not accepted by the AKC until 1976, although it is one of Britain's oldest breeds and originated in Scotland.

BEARDED COLLIE
Colors: Shades of gray and shades of brown
Height: 20"-22"
Weight: 55 – 65 lbs.

A Bearded Collie pup will probably be born a solid color, and the shading will come in as the pup grows. Some can be silver, others almost black, some cream and others dark brown.

It's possible that the breed came about when the Polish Lowland Sheepdog was bred with local sheepdogs in Scotland in the 16th century. It's been suggested that the Komondor from Hungary was added to the mix.

Beardies are energetic, happy, friendly dogs. They love children, and are totally devoted to their families. The pups have a particular sweetness about them that lasts throughout their lives. Like children, they love to play with their toys, and even have favorites that they carry around with them.

Because it's a very lively puppy, it should be allowed to scamper about for exercise. As an adult dog, it will need to release its boundless energy either in a fenced yard, or with long walks. It would certainly love to run free in the fields, and once your dog has learned recall, it will race back to your side on command. Beside you is one of this collie's favorite places to be.

Of course you'll have to teach the pup its manners, but it's not necessary to be too strict with this one. This is a dog that is anxious to please its owner. Because of their pleasant disposition, Beardies are often used as therapy dogs.

You'll have to groom its beautiful coat regularly – twice a week and will need professional help if you intend to show your dog. Some owners keep their companion dog's coat trimmed, but this would be a choice you would make.

The breed is generally healthy, and some Beardies live to fourteen years, but we should warn you that Addison's disease has shown up from time to time in this breed. If caught in time, Addison's can be treated with medication. If your dog goes off its food, and acts lethargic, you might want to get it tested for Addison's.

Now some of you may be looking for a small dog, and if so, the next breed suggested for you is special in many ways.

PEMBROKE WELSH CORGI
Colors: Red, sable, fawn, black and tan with or without white.
Height: 10" - 12"
Weight: 25 - 30lbs.

Beloved by the British royal family, the Pembroke Welsh Corgi has been a part of their family for decades. Queen Elizabeth owns several of them.

The breed's name comes from the Celt word for dog. Corgis came to Wales in the 12th century with Flemish weavers and the Welsh used the dogs for herding cattle. The little dogs nipped the heels of straying animals to keep them in line.

A Corgi would rather play than fight, and usually adores children. Nevertheless, it's still a watchdog, and is protective of its territory. Strangers will be treated with suspicion. *Socialize* your pup at its special imprint time of twelve weeks. Introduce it to as many strangers and other dogs as possible in pleasant circumstances. This will help the dog to be more relaxed when strangers come to your home.

You would be a good owner for this one, Scorpio, because at times the dog gets over excited, stimulated by hyperactive people. Your quiet handling of the dog, and your loving heart will keep the dog on a steady course. You won't have to persevere with its training though. Corgis learn their lessons earlier than most breeds, and if you want to show it as a young dog, it will behave well in the ring.

You'll need to brush and comb your dog a couple of times a week to keep its coat in good condition.

The Pembroke has an inquisitive nature, and loves to explore its neighborhood, town or country. Walks are important for this sturdy, hardy little dog.

The dog loves good food, and will beg to share it with you. It's hard not to give in to its charming manner of begging. The Pembroke has such an appealing little face, and very expressive eyes. Being overweight is a serious problem for all dogs, but more so for dogs with short legs. If you are aware of this, you'll be stricter with its diet to keep the dog healthy – well most of the time anyway.

It would be difficult not to fall for a Pembroke once it becomes a part of your family. It's a charming little dog with one aim in life – to please you.

The Pembroke has a cousin who is also a sweetheart – the **CARDIGAN WELSH CORGI.** It has a bushier tail, and bigger ears. Although similar in appearance, it is classified as a separate breed. The Celts brought the dog from Europe to Cardiganshire in Wales in the 12th century. Like the Pembroke, the dog was used on farms to herd cattle.

In temperament, the breed is less outgoing than its cousin, and is a quieter dog - less perky, but still ready for a game with a ball. If you want to show your dog, the Cardigan is very easy to prepare for the ring, and usually behaves well when traveling. It's a good breed for apartment living, but loves to go for a walk. There'll be no scrappy dogfights with this one as Cardigans behave with decorum.

The Pembroke is more popular on both sides of the Atlantic, but the Australians favor the loyal, faithful little Cardigan. Check them both out. Either one will win your heart.

Corgis are delightful little dogs, but if you are looking for a Toy, this one has a mystical past.

LHASA APSO
Colors: Honey, golden, dark grizzle, sandy, slate, smoke, black, white or brown.
Height: 10"-11"
Weight: 13 - 18lbs.

Some of you are interested in the occult, and are fascinated by interesting stories of the mystique. You may be intrigued to hear that the Lhasa Apso was considered to be a sacred dog in Tibet centuries ago, and was treated with great reverence. This little dog was a spiritual companion of priests and monks, and was hidden away from commoners until travelers brought the breed to Europe in the 1920's. Ancient beliefs claim that the souls of high priests entered into the bodies of Lhasa Apsos at the moment of death. Such beliefs gave Apsos great esteem. If you lived in Tibet, a gift of a Lhasa Apso would be a gift of good luck.

The Apso is a sweet and affectionate pet. Toss a ball or a squeaky toy, and the little dog scampers after it, delighted to have a chance to play with you.

You'll need to groom your dog's hair regularly – tangles really hurt. If you don't intend to show the dog, you can trim its coat to make it more manageable. The dog's expressive eyes are fringed with long lashes that help to keep its long hair from getting in the way of its vision. The breed has acute hearing, and lets you know when visitors are at the door, or there's an intruder.

Your lifestyle is important in that this little dog doesn't like to be alone for a long time. If you live alone, and are absent a great deal, we suggest you get a pair of Apsos. They will delight in each other's company except when it comes to sharing you.

The dog is social, but naturally wary of strangers. Small children can hurt this little pup without meaning to, and their jerky, fast movements can make the dog uneasy. It responds well to older children who understand the rules of handling its small frame. The dog is hardy, used to winters in the mountains, and has an inner coat along with its outer coat. However, respectful handling is good for this one.

You could get annoyed that your Lhasa Apso will choose to dig out a buried treasure in the yard just after you have bathed and groomed it, but this is all part of this sweetheart's charm, and if you can put up with that, who knows? You could get good luck just for having a Lhasa Apso in your life.

Now, for those of you who are extremely busy, and do not have the time to groom your Toy, perhaps this docile, non-demanding little dog would be right for you.

PUG
Colors: Silver, apricot, fawn with dark face, solid black.
Height: 10" – 11"
Weight: 14 - 18 lbs.

The Pug is one of the easiest dogs in the canine world to care for. It doesn't need a lot of exercise, its coat is short and smooth, so needs very little grooming, and it's a wonderful companion.

In Latin, the word "pugnus" means fist, and it's because this tiny look-alike to the huge Mastiff has a head like a clenched fist, it was named the Pug. Well, that's one theory as to its name. Another is that the dog was named after a Chinese word, as the dog originated in the Orient, and was the companion of the Emperors of China. Later, the breed was found in Japan, and then Europe. It was in the 1600's that Pugs were brought to England, and found favor with Queen Victoria, painters and sculptors. Today, it is favored for Show, and as a beloved member of the family.

You'll find that this small dog has an incredibly large heart. Its love for you will literally shine through its large expressive eyes, and from the first day you bring the pup home, you can resign yourself to being absolutely adored.

It would be impossible for some of you not to become equally fond of your Pug. Not only does it give you little trouble in or out of the home, it demands very little from you. Of course, a little exercise should be provided to keep its muscles in good tone, and you should keep those wrinkles in its coat clean. Long walks are not advised, although your Pug would try its best to keep up with you. If your dog wheezes, it's time to stop.

Pugs wait patiently for their chance to star at Show, and travel well. A happy Pug can look quite perky in the ring, so if you plan to go for Best, play with your pup and encourage it to be lively.

The smallest varieties of this breed can be delicate, and you should know that due to its short nose, your Pug will snore. Keep an eye on its diet, too, or your loving companion will pass odorous gas.

Generally, this little dog is easy-going and peaceful. True, it doesn't like to be pushed into anything, and can be quite stubborn if not handled in the right way, but a Pug obeys an owner it adores through its devotion. Some of you Scorpios will win this dog's heart totally, as it will surely win yours.

The Doberman, Akita, Bull Terrier, Labrador, Bearded Collie, Corgis, Lhaso Apso and the Pug are the breeds we suggest for your sun sign personality, Scorpio. We hope we have been of help to you.

Good luck in picking your perfect pup.

Doberman

Akita

Bull Terrier

Labrador
Retriever

Bearded Collie

Cardigan Welsh Corgi

Pembroke
Welsh
Corgi

Lhaso Apso

Pug

SAGITTARIUS THE ARCHER
November 23 through December 21

Tin is your metal
Your stone is topaz
Tomatoes are your plants
And your color is purple, also royal blue
Now let's find the pup that's right for you

"Does it ever move?" many of you might say, prodding a sleeping Bulldog gently with your foot. "What sort of dog is that to have about?" Well, even though it's a dog with a heart of gold, Sagittarius, it's not likely to be your kind of dog. Before we get into the breeds that would be right for you, though, it's important to us that you understand where we're coming from.

Initially, as a professional astrologer and a canine behaviorist, our first question was, "What kind of dog owner would a Sagittarius be?". We found the answer by thoroughly studying your sun sign personality. Once we knew what you would probably look for in a dog, we considered all of the breeds registered with the American Kennel Club to find some perfect pups for you. Now, we're not saying that you can only successfully own the dogs we have selected for you. What we are saying is that the pups we suggest would be good choices for your sun sign personality.

We'll first review the characteristics of your sun sign, and discuss dog traits and temperaments that could be a plus or a minus for you. Your compatible pups are then described in full so that you can make your own decision based upon your lifestyle and personal preference.

Your sign shows you to be an optimistic person. Full of enthusiasm, you race around life's corners, convinced that you will find something of interest at every turn. When you hit a blank wall, you won't stay disappointed for long. There's always another corner.

Most of you see little point in dwelling on the past. You prefer to embrace each day as a new adventure. Your positive energy can work magic at times, but this only surprises other people. You, Sagittarius, believe.

Many of you are very direct and out-spoken. It's rare that you'll beat around the bush in your speech or in your actions. Your enthusiastic approach to life has no yellow caution lights, and this is reflected in your dealings with people. You are usually outspoken on every issue, and tend to make your views known without checking on your listeners' reactions. You are sincere when you share your unvarnished truths, and rarely understand people's responses to some of them. You are surprised when they walk away from you, and then avoid you.

You are just as outspoken on vital subjects like man's inhumanity to man, careless oil spills polluting the oceans, killing the wildlife, freedom of choice, and the rights of all individuals to be equal, no matter how different they may be.

Finding out what's happening in our world is of great interest to many of you. You are inquisitive, and love to learn. Most of you thoroughly enjoy sharing your knowledge with others. New concepts stimulate you, especially if they have an awesome potential, but learning in a structured environment is not usually a choice you make. It's too restrictive and methodical for your restless, independent spirit.

Many of you are unconventional folk. Stuffy conventions, rules, regulations, what's politically correct or what's not holds your interest for a microsecond. What does any of that matter? You prefer a more broad-minded view. Differences intrigue you – not the same old boring patterns.

Of course, it follows that most of you resist routine. Anything that ties you to one thing in one place feels like a shackle. Freedom to come and go as you please is your inalienable right. You can be a super friend, Sagittarius, and a wonderful caring person in a deep relationship, but it must be your choice to bind yourself with emotional chains, and even then, you will sometimes balk at being tied down by them.

You are a free spirit, Sagittarius - an adventurer, full of positive energy that is often untamed. You fight for justice, are innately honest, and feel compassion for the underdog.

The name of your sign, Sagittarius the Archer, symbolizes the idealism and hope in your personality. You have several arrows for your bow and do not hesitate to shoot them.

Most of you have a special affinity with animals. People may often misunderstand you, but animals sense your warmth, and give you their trust and affection unconditionally. You probably feel some compassion for all unwanted dogs, and could even be involved in trying to stop their use in lab experiments, or be on a committee that makes sure humane procedures are practiced at animal shelters across the country. Cruelty of any sort incenses you, and when it comes to animals, some of you leap on your white horses and charge to their rescue.

Still, although you may feel protective towards the entire canine world, you wouldn't necessarily want to own a lot of the breeds. Your dog should be special in some way, unusual perhaps, or especially beautiful. Certainly you would like a dog you could be proud of. Most of you would like to be able to say, "That's my dog!" and burst a few buttons as you say it.

We'll now talk about the plus and minus breed traits for your Sagittarius personality to help you to choose a breed you can respond to with pride. Beautiful or unusual is great, but this is not all your dog should be. Some dogs are both, but they tune out, often preferring not to participate in activities with you. This would puzzle you, and then irritate you. If, in addition, the dog did not seek your love or return it in any great measure, you would be disappointed in your canine buddy.

Most of you are full of zest and spirit. Any dog with your last name on its collar tag should also be spirited, and embrace life with a similar enthusiasm. If you owned a placid dog, even if it was devoted to you, you might forget it was there half the time. You'd probably give it an affectionate nickname like "Dodo", and think up ways to spark some life into the dog. As amusing as this might be for some of you, temporarily, it would be better to get a breed with a spirited temperament.

Of course, some breeds have spirit, and are affectionate, but are just natural slow pokes. They only come to life when they scent game to track, and are a touch obsessive in their active state. Generally these dogs like to mull over your commands, and consider their options. You may smile affectionately as you jump over this laidback pooch, but you probably won't wait around for it to move. You have places to go, people to see, and things to do. Sometimes you'll take your dog with you, but only if it can keep up. An alert, eager companion is more for you.

So far we have attractive dogs, full of affection for you, spirited, lively, active breeds. However, your dog might be all of the above, but could also be aggressively protective. Many of you are outgoing, social people. Some of you chat to total strangers as though they were good friends. You even get into animated arguments with them. If your dog was a very possessive and protective breed, it could growl at any stranger who dared to raise his or her voice to you. The growl would warn. If the person became intense, and you became cross, this dog could decide enough was enough, move from the defensive to the offensive, and attack the upstart. At the time, you would probably commend the dog's intelligence. During the lawsuit, you might have a second thought or two. A friendly, social dog without tunnel vision where you're concerned would be a more compatible companion for you.

To sum up, Sagittarius, you have a fondness for all dogs, but would be happier owning a dog that is unusual or beautiful. Your dog should give you a sense of pride in the way it looks, and in the way it behaves. You would prefer an affectionate dog that has an adventurous spirit, and is quick and alert. However, your dog should not be too possessive of you or over-protective.

It should be a social breed – a dog that's friendly, and adds to the fun in your life.

As you consider the dogs suggested for you, give some thought to your lifestyle. For example, the first breed recommended for your personality needs daily exercise.

DALMATIAN
Colors: White with black or liver spots
Height: 19" - 24"
Weight: 40 – 60 lbs.

A Dalmatian is a high-spirited breed with a friendly, affectionate nature. The dog is well proportioned, and very attractive if you are into spotted dogs that actually grin at you. This dog will smile a lot at an enthusiastic owner who will take charge, but give praise and affection at the same time.

Authorities differ on this breed's origin. Some claim the dog comes from Dalmatia. Others suggest the dog is descended from the Hound of Bengal, and comes from the East.

Paintings of similar dogs have been found in old Egyptian tombs, running behind chariots, and have also been found on frescos done in the 15th century. In England, the dog protected horse-drawn carriages, traveling many, many miles. When the breed came to the U.S. it became the firemen's dog, ever ready to follow the horse-drawn fire tucks, and was soon famous for rescuing victims from burning buildings. Unfortunately for Dals, horsepower replaced horses. Riding in fire trucks just wasn't the same.

Dals love horses. If you don't ride yourself, don't be surprised if your Dal tries to join total strangers who trot by you in the park, or gallop passed you in the country. A Dal can be reserved with strangers, but every horse it meets is an instant friend.

Most of you won't find it hard to train this one because the dog is both bright and eager to please, but it's important to understand that your Dal has a restless spirit akin to your own. It needs to run and play more than most breeds, and if kept penned, could lose its spirit and its appetite. Most of you will understand this dog very well.

If you live in a city apartment, and rarely have the chance to escape concrete landscapes, a Dal would not be a good choice for you, Sagittarius. The suburbs, with a fenced yard, or the country would be best for this breed.

You must do your homework when choosing a breeder. *The Hundred and One Dalmatians'* book, and subsequent movies, along with Budweiser Clydesdale Horses with the ever-present Dalmatians, has made this much demanded dog a victim of careless over breeding. It's worth your time to get a true Dal.

All Dalmatian puppies are born white, and their spots do not come in until later. If you don't intend your dog for Show, it doesn't matter where the spot pattern is, but breeders have worked hard to perfect this. You should also know that some Dalmatians are born deaf, so it's a good idea to check on this when selecting your pup.

If your Dal loves the water, and you live by the ocean, be sure to wash off the salt – it can cause dermatitis and other allergies.

A Dal needs a strong, kind owner. When you reward its efforts, it will grow in spirit and ability. If you don't misunderstand its over-eagerness to please, and are patient with its clumsy puppy ways, you'll not only have a devoted, lively companion, you'll have a dog of which you can be truly proud.

Dalmatians are sweethearts, but if you're looking for a spectacularly beautiful dog, check out this one.

IRISH SETTER
Colors: Mahogany or rich chestnut red
Height: 25"- 27"
Weight: 50 – 70 lbs.

It's hard to find a more glamorous dog than this setter. When the sun shines off its rich-colored, silky coat, the dog is incredibly beautiful. You'll find it attracts attention wherever it goes, and enjoys the attention of even total strangers.

Spaniels, pointers and other setters are said to be in the making of the Irish Setter. At one time they came in red and white, but the solid red color was the preferred color for Show. The Irish Earl of Enneskillen wouldn't allow a red and white in his kennels, and contributed to red becoming the only color for an Irish.

There's always a price to be paid for a dog with a gorgeous full coat. Even if you don't intend your dog for Show, you should groom it regularly. Start brushing your dog as a pup, and make it a pleasant experience. For some of you this will be a chore, and you may consider passing it on to an-other family member. However, by brushing your dog, and talking quietly as you brush, you'll not only cement the bonding between you, you'll lower your blood pressure!

When the dog has attached to you, this setter performs extremely well in the field. It is swift, hardy and has an excellent sense of smell. It enjoys a hunt on wet or dry terrain. It's important to work the dog with an understanding, firm hand, though. The dog is highly-strung, and over-anxious to please. As a pup, it tries too hard, misunderstands, and makes mistakes. Any harsh, punitive handling would ruin its potential. Fortunately, Sagittarius, you treat each day as a new beginning. The pup's mistakes of yesterday will be history. Your innate understanding of animals, combined with your interest in teaching, will undoubtedly bring out the best in this pup. You certainly won't be "soft" with the dog, but you'll give it lots of chances, which is just what an Irish Setter needs to be a champion. *Socialize* your pup when it's twelve weeks old – the special imprint time for all pups. Introduce it to as many friendly adults, children, and other dogs as you can in pleasant circumstances. It will help the excitable dog to be more relaxed when strangers are about for the rest of its life.

It's a good watchdog, barking to warn you of approaching visitors. Of course, the Irish Setter is such a friendly dog, it could be giving them a verbal welcome, but at least you'll know someone is outside your door.

Like the Dalmatian (see above), an Irish Setter needs lots of exercise. This is a dog you can take on a long hike, and it'll be you that'll need a rest long before the dog. Alert, bright, and ever eager to explore, the dog quivers with anticipation the moment you pick up its leash.

The dog is an excellent family dog, but might be a bit boisterous with tots in its eagerness to play. It has such a sweet nature that, if handled correctly, it's a wonderful therapy dog. If you take the time this one needs, you'll own an outstanding breed of extreme beauty, which is just what some of you are looking for.

If you like the Irish Setter's spirit, but favor curly tops, this one might interest you.

IRISH WATER SPANIEL
Color: Rich liver
Height: 20" - 23"
Weight: 50 - 60 lbs.

The Irish Setter, Poodle, and water spaniels are in the recipe for this ancient breed. It was first shown in 1877. The dog is well known for its endurance and stamina in the sport of hunting waterfowl. Because it has a completely waterproof coat, the Irish Water Spaniel can work in freezing cold waters for hours on end, and has a lively, eager attitude towards its work.

Training this one is not difficult because it's naturally obedient, and is an intelligent dog. Irish Water Spaniels have playful, affectionate temperaments. They are loyal and loving to their families, and are particularly good with children who have not handled them roughly.

If you don't hunt, your dog will thoroughly enjoy retrieving games, and long walks. Most Irish Water Spaniels love the water, and regular swimming actually helps the dog's ringlets to grow correctly.

You'll need to comb the dog's hair a couple of times a week to avoid matting, and cut its coat every couple of months to keep it looking smart.

If you want to show your dog, you'll need a professional.

Ear problems are known to affect this breed, and it can be sensitive to sulfa drugs or to some forms of anesthesia. Be sure that your vet is familiar with the breed.

The country or the suburbs with a fenced yard is best for this dog. It delights in the smells of the country, to swim, and to run by your side as an excellent hunting partner, or as a loyal and devoted companion.

Dalmatians, Irish Setters, and Irish Water Spaniels are special dogs, each in their own way, but here's an outstanding breed of a different kind.

SIBERIAN HUSKY
Colors: Wolf gray, silver gray shadings, sable to black
Height: 20 "- 23"
Weight: 45 - 60 lbs.

A close relative of the wolf, the Siberian Husky was developed as a sled dog by the Chukchis, who lived in northeastern Asia. When the early Russian explorers came to Alaska, they used them because of their speed over snow and ice. Nansen and Peary favored them also when they explored the territory. The breed quickly gained a good reputation, but really became famous worldwide when they raced against time to deliver serum to stop the outbreak of diphtheria in Nome. Recognition of the breed by the U.S. was achieved in 1930.

The Husky attracts attention wherever it goes because of its striking appearance. Its almond-shaped eyes are set in a well-furred face, and it's a graceful canine. These members of the spitz family are compact, agile, swift on their feet, and have incredible endurance.

Although their coats are extremely dense, and can withstand the coldest of temperatures, Huskies are very adaptable, and can live anywhere, indoors or out. They are amiable companions. One of the plus factors of this breed is that Siberian Huskies are usually healthy, and require little nurturing. Of course, they love the winter, and even older Huskies behave like puppies when they can bound over ground covered with snow.

Grooming this dog is an easy chore, with regular brushing to keep the dog's coat in good condition. Brushing its coat helps to cement the bonding between you and the pup. Like most Spitz breeds, Huskies are not possessive of their owners. When they attach, they are faithful and protective. Your enthusiasm and positive handling of this breed will help the bonding process, and your obvious admiration and affection will cement it.

Remember that if you kennel your Husky outside, keep the contact frequent. Unlike some breeds that assume you need them, your Husky will need to be shown that often.

Socialize your adorable furry pup at the age of twelve weeks, which is the special imprint time for all pups. Introduce the dog to as many friendly adults, children, and other dogs as you can in pleasant surroundings. Socialization will not change a Husky's protective instincts. It will make the dog friendlier to admiring strangers when it knows they mean no harm. It's almost impossible to walk a Husky without some passing stranger pausing to admire the dog. It's a very distinctive breed.

All of the suggested breeds discussed above do their jobs well as watchdogs, but if you are looking for a serious guard dog, this one can be quite formidable.

BOUVIER DES FLANDRES
Colors: Fawn to black, pepper and salt, gray and brindle
Height: 24.5"– 27.5"
Weight: 80 – 90 lbs.

The French word "bouvier" means cowherd, and herding cattle for farmers and butchers in France and Flanders was the Bouvier's main work. The Bouvier has been called many names in the past, such as Toucheur de Boeuf (cattle driver), Koe Hond (cow dog), and Vuilbaard (dirty beard). The breed was almost wiped out in World War I when the fighting was intense, and the cattle dog became a war dog. It was used to carry messages through enemy lines, and beloved for its rescue of wounded men on the field of battle. Enough survived to breed the Bouvier of today. The AKC recognized the breed in 1929.

This strong, agile, intelligent canine has continued to work as an army dog. The police also recruit it. It's an excellent guard dog, and its even temperament has made the dog successful as a guide dog for the blind. In South Africa, Bouviers are used for junior jockey miniature sulkie races.

Because you are a social person, Sagittarius, it is important that you *socialize* your Bouvier pup at twelve weeks, which is its special imprint time. Introduce the pup to as many adults, children and other dogs as possible in pleasant surroundings. Bouviers focus on their guarding work with intense concentration, and can be formidable dogs.

How aggressive this dog will be is entirely up to you, Sagittarius. Left to its own devices, the dog views all strangers as potential foes. Under your positive, affectionate but strong hand, the dog will do well. It's your upbeat approach to life that will bring out the lighter, fun side of this loyal, protective dog. With the right guidance, the Bouvier will be docile and obedient in the family home.

Give the dog a regular brushing and combing for more than one reason. Start brushing your dog when it's a pup. It will keep the tangles out of its coat, and importantly, teach the dog who is Alpha – the leader of its pack. You will be taking over where its mother left off, and there's no doubt in the pup's mind who controlled who in that relationship!

Some of you will appreciate this dog's powerful physique, its curly hair, and its excellent guarding abilities, but all of you will like the intelligent, affectionate look in its dark eyes. It's a very good guard dog and a lovable companion.

The next breed that we suggest for you, Sagittarius, is a remarkable breed of true distinction.

GERMAN SHEPHERD
Colors: Black, black and tan, gray
Height: 22" - 26"
Weight: 77 - 95 lbs.

If you choose a true German Shepherd pup, you'll be the owner of a breed hailed as a champion all over the world. Shepherds are spirited, resilient, intelligent, and learn with an alert eagerness.

Shepherds are very trainable by good handlers, which is why the police, military and customs recruit them. They are also in great demand as guide dogs for the blind as they are capable of being very loyal, and are usually devoted to their owners. In addition to their utilitarian value, they are also superb show dogs, and have taken home the champion's cup on both sides of the Atlantic.

Firm, direct, positive training is the way to go with this pup, but you'll have to find the time for serious training. It's a dominant breed, and needs your leadership and direction.

Left to its own devices, with only intermittent training, the dog could decide for itself as to who and what to dominate. Of course, it's not likely that you'll allow this to happen. It's a rare Sagittarius who takes orders from a family member. Besides, when you have an achiever like a Shepherd, it's both challenging and exciting to train the pup to its full potential.

As its name suggests, the breed is German, and was first brought to the U.S. post World War I by soldiers returning home. Since then the dog has become extremely popular. When quantity and not quality is sought, blood-lines suffer. Many of you are impulsive. *Don't buy the first pup you find unless you have checked on both the breeder and the pup's background.* With a little extra effort, you can find a real purebred.

German Shepherds shed. You'll need to brush the dog regularly. There are two important reasons why you should do this yourself. Brushing your Shepherd will strengthen the growing bond between you, and the action of brushing and stroking your dog can lower your blood pressure. Although most of you rarely give more than a passing thought to such things, you'll be helping both you and the dog to stay healthy.

When your pup is about three months old, it's important to *socialize* it with as many friendly adults, children and dogs as you can in pleasant circumstances. Twelve weeks is the dog's special imprint time. *Socialization* will not affect the dog's natural guarding instincts, but it will help the dog to be more at ease with strangers for the rest of its life.

Since you love to chat with total strangers, Sagittarius, it's important for the dog to be able to distinguish friend from foe, stranger or not, especially if you get into an argument.

This dog has a noble look, and is a beautiful dog. If you train it with firmness, and kindness, and have chosen the right breeder, you'll definitely own a champion.

So far all of your suggested pups are a fair size, but perhaps you're looking for a smaller dog. If so, check out the 2008 winner of the Best in Show at Westminster.

BEAGLE
Colors: White with black and tan saddle markings.
Height: 13"-16"
Weight: 18 -30 lbs.

Originally an English hunting dog, the Beagle packs ran with the hounds. It hasn't forgotten foxes and other game are about for the chase, and enters into the whole business with quivering excitement. Well, the Beagle enters into most things in this way. It's a very happy, eager little dog with an optimistic outlook on life. This is probably why the breed has an excellent reputation for living to a ripe old age.

Instant obedience is just not one of the Beagle's best points. It's as independent as you are, Sagittarius, and resists being interrupted when busy. However, it's a very lovable, mischievous little dog with a very affectionate nature. If you raise the pup with a loving, firm hand, and win its loyalty, you'll also solve the obedience problem – well, most of the time.

You don't have to live in the country to have a happy Beagle. It's very adaptable, and good for the suburbs or apartment living. Of course, one of the first things it may learn is where you keep its leash, and bring it to you the moment you walk in the door.

The Beagle's coat is short and smooth, but brushing the dog will help to keep it shiny. You should watch your dog's diet, though. The pup will soon learn who munches the most in your family, and comes equipped with charming begging skills.

A Beagle is not hard to show because the dog's lively temperament and keen interest in everything that's going on helps it to show well. It loves to be part of a family, and is good with children. It also loves playmates of its own breed. Lyndon B. Johnson owned three Beagles named Him, Her, and Edgar.

Most people who have owned Beagles stay faithful to the breed. It is trained through affection, returns the affection with devotion, and is usually lots of fun to live with. It will go wherever you go, Sagittarius, and every outing will be viewed with extreme excitement. Some of you will absolutely adore this one.

Perhaps, though, you're looking for a small terrier breed. If so, here's one with a different, distinctive look.

DANDIE DINMONT
Colors: Pale gray to black or fawn to rich gold
Height: 8"-10"
Weight: 18 – 24 lbs.

Many crossings of Sky Terriers and Scottish Terriers produced this one. The gypsies favored the breed for its loyal, protective nature and easy adaptability to new places. The little dog is quite willing to go along wherever you go. Its loyalty remains with you. Although it's an old breed, it wasn't until the early 1800's that Dandies became popular. Sir Walter Scott, who bred them, included the dog in one of his novels, *Guy Mannering*, and the dog was named after the protagonist in the novel, a farmer named Dandie Dinmont, who kept six of these terriers.

For a small dog, the Dandie Dinmont has lots of courage, and does not fear the unknown. It's usually polite to strangers, but is an excellent watchdog for the home. Its deep bark gives the impression of a much larger dog on guard.

Dandies are different in appearance to most terriers, and are quieter and calmer than most. True to its type, though, this dog chooses its favorite person as a pup, and remains loyal for the rest of its life.

Perhaps what many of you will like about this little dog, Sagittarius, is the expression in the dog's eyes. It not only shows its intelligence, it's an honest look, as though affirming your decision to trust it. Being devious is not in this dog's nature – no sneaky moves – but it does have a cheeky sense of humor that you'll soon get to know.

Like most of you, a Dandie loves its freedom. Once the dog has control over its bladder and bowels, don't cage this one. It should have the freedom of its home to romp in. You'll soon have a depressed dog if you lock the dog up in a confined space.

You'll need to comb the dog's coat at least twice a week, and when adult, the dog will need to see a professional a couple of times a year for hand stripping. This is important for a Dandie, as if you do not take care of its grooming needs, the dog will have to be stripped down to its skin, and will look very odd for a long time.

Many of you would love the hunting spirit in a Dandie, but a word of warning. Dandies consider skunk catching as part of their reason for being in this world. If you live where skunks are plentiful, stock up on tomato juice to combat the skunks' stinky counter-attacks. Your Dandie will also love to chase squirrels, so you should have a fenced yard if you live in the suburbs.

This breed has taken Best in Show on both sides of the Atlantic, and there's no doubt in our minds that if you want a small dog, this one is a big winner in all ways.

The Dalmatian, Irish Setter, Irish Water Spaniel, Siberian Husky, Bouvier des Flandres, German Shepherd, Beagle, and Dandie Dinmont are the breeds we suggest for your sun sign personality, Sagittarius. We hope we have been of help to you.

Good luck in picking your perfect pup.

Dalmatian

Irish Setter

Irish Water Spaniel

Siberian Husky

Bouvier des Flandres

German Shepherd

Beagle

Dandie Dinmont

CAPRICORN THE GOAT
December 22 - January 20

Lead is your metal
Your stone is turquoise
Pansies are your flowers
And your colors are black, brown, gray – all dark
Now let's find that pup with a Capricorn bark

"You must be joking?" many of you would say if we handed you a pink Chinese Crested dog, hairless except for its white powder-puff hat, and tufts on its tail and feet. "Is this a dog?" you may question dubiously. Absolutely. It's a lively, sweet little dog, Capricorn, but it's not likely to be your kind of dog. Before we get into which breeds would be right for you, though, it's important to us that you understand where we're coming from.

Initially, as a professional astrologer and a canine behaviorist, our first question was, "What kind of dog owner would a Capricorn be?". We found the answer by thoroughly studying your sun sign personality. Once we knew what you would probably look for in a dog, we considered all of the breeds registered with the American Kennel Club to find some perfect pups for you. Now, we're not saying that you can only successfully own the dogs we have selected for you. What we are saying is that the pups we suggest would be good choices for your sun sign personality.

We'll first review the characteristics of your sun sign, and discuss dog traits and temperaments that could be a plus or a minus for you. Your compatible pups are then described in full so that you can make your own decision based upon your lifestyle and personal preference.

Your sign shows you to be a dependable person, reliable and trustworthy. You look to your home and to your family, and are conscientious in their care. No matter what comes down in your life, for yourself or for your loved ones, you see it through with endurance. The wisdom you were born with develops over the years, but for some of you, there are many inward struggles, and your path is difficult, strewn with obstacles.

Loyal to the extreme, your immediate family will always come first. You'll demand respect from them, and obedience from the younger members, but you'll be devoted to them. When the kids grow up and seek their freedom, it's sometimes difficult for you to let them go, as you will no longer be able to protect them from the outside world. Some of you will feel the empty-nest syndrome strongly, but you endure this hardship as you do most things.

Although when you are younger, you tend to be unsure of yourself, this changes with maturity. Throughout your life the traditional ways feel more comfortable to you, but you are also pragmatic. If new advancements improve on the old systems, you'll adopt them. They must be proven, though. Claims of greatness will not be enough for most of you.

Looking on the bright side is not part of your personality. It's difficult for most of you to be optimistic. You are much too realistic to depend on dreams and possibilities. In fact, you rarely accept anything at face value, and remain suspicious.

It follows, then, that most of you will tend to look on the dark side, especially when you are feeling at odds with yourself, and the rest of the world. Full of doom and gloom, you can turn a sunny day dark. Fortunately, your practical nature soon gets you up and going again.

Well, if the world were full of Capricorns, con games would surely become extinct. You would be a rare Capricorn if you have fallen prey to con artists. Even compliments are suspect to most of you. You certainly don't accept them gracefully, although you need some verbal appreciation just like everybody else.

Many of you are of the opinion that the good things in life should be earned through hard work, and you are willing to do more than your fair share. It's not likely that you'll be obvious or flamboyant in your efforts. That's not your style. You take your work seriously, and are quietly dedicated to making a success of it. A strong sense of duty is an integral part of you, Capricorn. It would really bother most of you if you were unable to fulfill your obligations. This is why you tend to worry quite a bit, and to take life too seriously, but it's also why you are such a reliable and dependable person.

Your cautious nature comes through in most of your undertakings, and applies to your reactions to others. For example, you're not likely to lavish praise on anyone, even if they have accomplished something significant, and you are truly delighted by it. When the rest of their friends hear about it, and are using words like "tremendous," "super", "incredible", and "wonderful", your comment would likely be, "That's good," which for you means all of the above.

Some of you do have another side. There will be days when you'll throw your cares aside, and embrace the ridiculous. On such days you both surprise and amuse your friends.

Many of you love a good arguement. You'll rarely back down on issues of importance to you. You are often irritatingly correct too, and concede little. This wins you the arguement, but you can lose the friend because you tend to say it exactly like it is without too much thought to the other person's feelings.

As a mature adult, you prefer to have the controlling hand on shared endeavors. If your partner messes up, you would be furious. Your anger can be volcanic in its intensity because you seek perfection.

Your sign's name, "Capricorn the Goat", symbolizes your upward climb on stony paths, your endurance, and survival. Ruled by Saturn, the planet of limitation, restriction, and control, you are usually disciplined and methodical in your day-to-day approach to life. You gradually develop the wisdom with which you were born, and many of you live to a ripe enough age to pass it on.

When it comes to owning a dog, most of you will accept the responsibility it entails, and will probably read all about each recommended pup with interest. You rarely undertake any task lightly, and this will apply to owning a dog. We have selected breeds that you'll respect, but your dog will have to prove itself to you before you make it a member of your family. Then, woes betide anyone who harms a hair on its head!

Although most signs are cautioned to pick a dog suitable for their lifestyles, most of you will put this into the priority category immediately. Usually practical, you are not likely to want a ball of fluff if you live in the country, or a spirited, restless breed if you live in an apartment in the city.

Let's now look at aspects of dog owning most of you probably wouldn't appreciate. We'll also explore breed traits, and temperaments that would be a plus or a minus for you.

Most of you would scoff at the need to pamper, curl, and powder your pooch. You would also resist the temptation to rush out and choose pastel shades of ribbons for its curls. For you, it's a dog, not an ornament, and should look and behave like one.

Some of you admire aristocracy, and would be pleased by impressive bloodlines and champion stock. You'll take pride in a champion breed, but realistically, only if the purebred is a sensible dog, able to perform well.

Many of you love the country, and thoroughly enjoy long walks in the woods or in the parks. A heavyset dog, unable to keep up with you would not be likely to receive sympathy from you, and you're not likely to want to carry it home. You have a nurturing nature, but you're not normally indulgent.

It's also important for many of you to have a companion on your walks that will not turn the walk into a high-speed chase. You won't find it amusing to tear through the woods or streets chasing a dog headed the wrong way. When you call your dog, it should come back to your side, and most of you will train it to do so. Some breeds are not going to do this, though, even if you train them from dawn to sunset. Of course, it's not personal on their part, but that's not likely to be a factor in their favor where you're concerned.

It's a debate you're sure to lose, Capricorn, if you choose to get into it. It would be wiser to get a dog that not only attaches to you, but also can be trained to remember your rules.

You respect intelligence, high performance potential, and down-to-earth behavior from your dog. Some of you will look for a spirited playfulness in your pup, also. In your lighter moods, you will thoroughly enjoy a game with your canine buddy, and if the dog won't play, that's no fun at all. It should be a traditional dog, but one that will respond to playtime with enthusiasm.

A strong-spirited dog will not be a problem for most of you. You control with a firm, steady hand, and it's not likely that you'll accept bad behavior from your pup. However, a very sensitive breed, needing lots of cuddles and praise to develop well, could be a problem for you. You have a warm heart, but it's not likely that you'd be interested in coping with your dog's anxious temperament.

Well, so far we have eliminated the breeds that need lots of fancy grooming, chubbies that find a one-block walk hard going, dogs that take off like streaks of lightening at the first opportunity, breeds who find games beneath their dignity, and highly-strung dogs requiring special psychological handling. Of course, your occasional skittish moods will not extend to appreciating skittish dogs. Airheads are definitely out.

There is another important thing to consider when choosing your dog, Capricorn. Many of you fill your life with duty and devotion to your families. Family members do not always return this, and it would be nice to be on the receiving end when it comes to your dog. This is why we have selected some outstanding breeds capable of giving you life-long devotion and protection. Most of you certainly deserve it.

The first breed discussed would be perfect for some of you.

GERMAN SHORTHAIR POINTER
Colors: Liver or ticked
Height: 21" – 25"
Weight: 55 – 70 lbs.

Every inch an aristocrat, the German Shorthair Pointer has a powerful, well-balanced body, is capable of great endurance, is intelligent, and trains well in obedience. This one is the result of years of careful, selective breeding by German breeders to produce a fine, versatile dog.

Although the breed is believed to be first bred in the 1700's from Spanish pointers, the English Pointer, and Foxhounds, it was not brought to the U.S. until around 1920, where it soon became known as an excellent sporting breed. The dog can work with pheasant, quail, waterfowl, coons, possum and deer.

If you don't hunt, this breed is a wonderful house pet because it's clean, has an affectionate, mild disposition, and gets along very well with children, although a bit exuberant at times with tots. Because of Pointers' trainability, they are successful guide dogs for the blind. Protective of loved ones, they also make good watchdogs.

Showing this dog is very gratifying, and its performance in Field Trials is outstanding. However, if you intend to show the dog, and keep it as a pet, it's important to *socialize* your pup at the age of twelve weeks, which is the special imprint time for all pups. Introduce the dog to as many adults, children and other dogs as you can in pleasant surroundings. This will help your dog, when it matures, to be less suspicious of strangers, and to be more relaxed when strangers are about for the rest of its life. It will not affect its natural watchdog abilities.

Grooming this one is not a chore – brush with a good bristle bush, and to bring out the shine in the dog's coat, you can use a piece of chamois leather. If the dog goes into the ocean to swim, rinse off the salt to avoid dermatitis.

The country or the suburbs is a better home for this breed. It needs lots of exercise and is tireless on long hikes. Lack of exercise may make the dog restless. Owners have told us that it's the best dog in the whole world and a paragon of virtue. Of course, Capricorn, you're not likely to take their word on this, but if you pick a pup from a reputable breeder, we think you'll agree with them. Most of you love an aristocrat.

GERMAN WIREHAIR POINTERS may also appeal to you. It's believed that the Pudelpointer and the Polish Water Dog were added to the mix to achieve this remarkable sporting breed. The additional grooming needed for the German Wirehair is brushing more often, and occasionally the dog's coat should be stripped. This dog is extremely popular in Germany and in Scandinavian countries. Breeders wanted a dog that could sustain very bad weather, and to be able to track wilder game. A German Wirehair Pointer can dispatch a wild cat without hesitation. It may be more aggressive than the Shorthair Pointer, but you can handle this due to its excellent trainability.

The next breed suggested for your personality, Capricorn, is the most popular dog on both sides of the Atlantic.

LABRADOR RETRIEVER
Colors: Black, chocolate, yellow
Height: 21"-24"
Weight: 55 - 80 lbs.

Originally Labs were bred on the island of Newfoundland, which is now a province of Newfoundland and Labrador, Canada. Some authorities claim that the dog was once named the St. John's dog, and was used to help the fishermen in the St. John's area of Newfoundland. Others say that the Newfoundland was the St. John's dog, but the Labrador definitely has a Newfoundland in its mix. The British are credited with developing the breed we know today.

This dog's talents cover a broad range. The breed is used for hunting, tracking, retrieving, police work, search and rescue, guide dogs, aids for the disabled, agility and obedience.

If you are looking for a hunting dog, this one is tireless in the field and excellent in water. It ignores bad weather conditions, and has an obvious love of the sport. If you do not hunt, your dog might do some hunting on its own. Our Lab, Hector, often brought us a live pheasant or a duck when we were out walking in the fields. Carried in his soft mouth, the birds were complaining, but unharmed. The same dog could also be counted on to bring us the children's escaped guinea pigs and hamsters that only he could find, and they were always unharmed when he dropped them into the children's laps.

Retrieving something, anything, and bringing it to you is often the way this dog shows its love for you. When you come home, your Lab will probably bring you a present. Now this could be anything within its reach, maybe a shoe, a hat, glove or a sock, and it will be presented to you with barely-contained joy. It would be unwise to try to change this trait, Capricorn, as the dog will not understand. The dog pleases the hunter when it retrieves a bird, and the trait is ingrained. If you'd like to keep your shoes, gloves or socks in pairs, keep a couple of the dog's toys by the front and back doors. Your dog will present those to you quite happily as your welcome-home gift.

The bond between you will grow quickly, and the pup will scamper after you from room to room. The pup needs to attach, and it will develop well with an affectionate and companionable owner. Left too much on its own, without human companionship, it could become depressed, and then positively mournful if things do not improve. Even though psychology is not your strong suit, Capricorn, your attachment to your dog will ensure this does not happen.

Children and Labs get along very well, and the dog likes most adults. They can be quite choosy about being friends with just any dog, though, and can be aggressive to visiting canines. Socialize your pup at its special imprint time of three months with as many friendly adults, children and other dogs as you can in pleasant surroundings. This will help the dog to be less suspicious of strangers to your home, but will not affect its watchdog traits.

Training with physical punishment is not necessary. The tone of your voice works wonders with this one. Labs are proud to please you. When the pup does well, be sure to give it a dog treat along with your praise.

It's important to exercise your Lab, and if you have a backyard, it should be fenced. Grooming its coat is not difficult, using a good bristle brush should do it, but if you live by the ocean, and the dog is constantly in the water, wash off the salty water at the end of the day to avoid dermatitis.

If you remember that puppy stages last longer in larger breeds, a Lab can be everything you want in a dog.

It will turn inside out to please you and rarely, if ever, let you down.

Another sporting breed with a huge following is our next suggestion for you.

GOLDEN RETRIEVER
Colors: Pale cream to gold
Height: 21.5" - 24"
Weight: 60 -75lbs.

Some authorities claim that the Golden is a cross between Russian Sheepdogs and British Bloodhounds. One story goes an English breeder by the name of Lord Tweedmouth, who owned an estate on the Tweed River, purchased eight Russian sheepdogs in the mid-1800's. He bred them with bloodhounds to increase their scenting ability, and produced the Golden we know today. Another authority believes that Lord Tweedmouth, mixed the local Tweed Yellow Water Spaniel with an Irish Setter and English Blood-hound to achieve the Golden Retriever.

However this breed was achieved, the Golden Retriever is a beautiful dog with an intelligent, obedient, loyal and faithful nature. It's easy to train, and once the dog has been trained, it rarely forgets to stay on task. The Golden is a winner in Obedience, at Field Trials, as a guide dog for the blind, as an assist dog for the disabled, as a search and rescue dog, and in many other fields.

It's an excellent sporting breed, retrieving tirelessly from land or water regardless of weather conditions.

Although the dog works reliably in the worst of weathers, it's not good at weathering harsh treatment. A Golden has a sensitive nature and an overwhelming need to please its owner. It will certainly stay out of your way if you are not in a good mood. When it needs to bother you, the dog will gently paw your knee to attract your attention.

This dog is exceptionally popular, Capricorn, because of its amiable temperament. It loves children, and is an excellent housedog. Why we think it would be a good dog for you is because this is a dog that needs an owner who truly needs the dog. When neglected, and not given enough love and attention, the dog can go off its food and droop in spirit.

You'll need to brush your dog's longhaired coat often as it sheds. It's a good idea to start grooming your Golden when it's a pup. Make it a pleasant experience. The Golden loves to be brushed by a loving hand, and the bond between you will grow quickly.

This breed can be left at home alone, but be prepared for a big welcome when you come home, and a present. Your dog will grab the nearest thing to hand to give you. The trait is instilled from when hunters praised the dog for retrieving downed quail. If you don't want a closet filled with odd shoes, try keeping some of the dog's toys close to the front and back doors of your home.

Although the Golden is not an aggressive dog, it's advisable to *socialize* it at its special imprint time of twelve weeks by introducing it to as many strangers, and other dogs as possible. Socialization will help your dog to be more comfortable in your absences in the care of strangers, and to be more confident in strange places for all of its life.

It really doesn't matter where you live if you own a Golden. The dog adapts to country town and city life. It loves a romp on the beach, or in the woods. Exercise is important as it's a sporting breed, and it absolutely loves to go for walks. If you live near the ocean, and the dog plays in the salt water, be sure to hose off the salt at the end of the day to avoid dermatitis. Your Golden will love to travel with you by car also, and up for anything you have in mind. Once your dog attaches to you, it wants to be wherever you are. It's a very loyal and devoted dog.

Pointers, Labradors, and Goldens are wonderful all-purpose breeds, but perhaps you are looking for a terrier of both substance and size. If so, check out this one.

KERRY BLUE TERRIER
Colors: Steel blue, blue-gray
Height: 17"- 19"
Weight: 33 - 40 lbs.

Known in its native country, Ireland, for over a century as the Irish Blue, the Kerry is an excellent companion and watchdog, and adapts well to city, town or country living, although exercise is a must for this muscular canine.

The dog was used to keep down the rat population on farms, to herd cattle, and to hunt from land or water in its native home, County Kerry. It's a very good swimmer.

One of the disadvantages when choosing your Kerry pup is that all pups are born black, and its color shading does not come in for about eighteen months. If you don't intend to show the dog, this is not important. A solid black Kerry, or one without the deep blue color, still makes a super protective, loyal friend.

The Kerry Blue sheds very little. However, it has a dense coat that needs to be brushed on a regular basis, and a professional should trim the dog's coat about three times a year or it will look very unkempt.

Like most terriers, the Kerry is an extrovert. It loves to know what is going on with everybody in the family, and it joins in whether invited to or not. A firm hand is needed to control the pup right from the start, and your usual no-nonsense manner is good for a Kerry. Of course, it will love your playful moods, and respond to them with much enthusiasm.

In Ireland, the Kerry can still be seen guarding, and herding the flock. When you adopt a Kerry, its job will be guarding you and your family and property. It can be aggressive to strangers, particularly other canines. This is why you should *socialize* the pup at its special imprint time of twelve weeks by introducing it to as many adults, children and other dogs as you can in pleasant surroundings. This will help your dog to be less suspicious of visitors who come to call. It will in no way affect its protective instincts.

The Kerry Blue is a family dog. It loves human company, particularly children. The dog is loyal, affectionate and playful. Some of you would love to add this one to your family.

Pointers, Labradors, Goldens, and Kerry Blues are great dogs in their own ways, but perhaps you are looking for a furry dog. If so, this one has both character and style.

KEESHOND
Colors: Shades of gray, cream undercoat
Height: 16"-19"
Weight: 55 - 65lbs.

Keeshonds are beautiful canines. Their coats are thick and their plumed tails curl over their backs. The dog has distinctive eyes. They are framed in fine lines on both sides of its face, running from the outer corners of its eyes to the lower corners of its ears. Some have said it looks like it's wearing specs.

The breed is a German Spitz, possibly coming from the Arctic originally, but is known as the Dutch barge dog. Keeshonds traveled the Rhine on barges to and from the Nethlands, serving as both companions and watchdogs. The breed's name is linked with Cornelius (Kees) de Gyzelaar, who led the patriots prior to the French Revolution. Kees' Spitz dog became the symbol of that revolt.

The Keeshond is intelligent, trains through attachment, and because of its acute hearing, is an excellent watchdog. There is an independent, proud air about the Keeshond. It needs a firm hand, but it also needs to know it is loved and respected by its owner. You prefer to be in control, Capricorn, and your dog will not have a problem with this. It needs a leader, but it does not want to be pampered or fussed over - something most of you are not likely to do. However, your praise is important, especially when the dog does well as a pup. Your approval is important to the dog's well being. Actually, Capricorn, this dog may get more response from you than most. When it looks to you for approval, it has such an endearing expression; you're sure to soften, and when you do you'll see a smile on the pup's face. It's often been called "the smiling Dutchman".

Groom the dog's beautiful coat by brushing it once a week. Start this when you bring the puppy home. It's good way to bond with the pup, and to send the message of who is in control. Its mother had the job of grooming it, and the pup remembers who was in charge when she did so. If you, Capricorn, are the one who teaches the dog its manners, grooms it, feeds it, and walks it you'll have a faithful and affectionate protector beside you.

Although the dog relates well to its family, it's not often outgoing, and like most of you, will usually be suspicious of the unknown. *Socialize* the pup at its special imprint time of three months. It will help the dog to be more social, and will not affect its protective traits. This is particularly important if you intend to show your Keeshond.

Housing this one outside is only okay if constant contact is made with the dog. Exercise is very important, and due to the dog's natural guarding traits, a fenced yard is preferable.

A Keeshond weathers cold temperatures well, but can be distressed in hot climates – it has such a thick, heavy coat of fur.

If you have children, your Keeshond will be good with them provided that they have not mishandled the dog when it was a pup. In fact, children are good for this breed, as they will bring out the playfulness in the dog.

It will choose its most important person early, and will be loyal and devoted. Some of you will feel the same about your handsome Keeshond.

Perhaps, though, you are looking for a smaller dog. This one doubles as a pet and a watchdog.

SCOTTISH TERRIER

Colors: Black, sandy or grizzle
Height: 10' – 11"
Weight: 18 – 23 lbs.

Exactly what went into the makings of a Scottish Terrier is not certain. The little terrier has been around since the 17th century. It was once known as the Aberdeen Terrier and its job was to flush foxes from their hideouts in the rocky terrain of Scotland. The breed came to the U.S. in 1883.

The Scottie became famous in America for two reasons. Many loved Fala, President Franklin D. Roosevelt's constant companion, and a Scottie became a familiar sight in advertisements for Scottish whiskey. Once people got to know the breed personally, its spirited and loyal nature spoke for itself. It's a popular pet, show dog, and watchdog.

Scottish Terriers have alert, intelligent expressions, and are particularly attentive to the sound of your voice. As a pup, a fly buzzing about will distract it from its lessons. Scotties are acutely inquisitive about everything in their lives, and the dog will really need to chase that fly! You'll have to be patient with this one, Capricorn, until it settles down to the business at hand. Most of you have lots of perseverance in your personality, and will have no problem with a Scottie pup. Those who have worked with the breed find the dog very trainable, and the scores at Obedience Trials for Scotties attest to their potential.

The dog's wiry coat will need grooming, and in order to keep the dog's characteristic shape, its coat will require a trim a couple of times a year.

Most Scotties are suspicious of strangers so *socialize* your pup at the age of twelve weeks, the special imprint time for all pups. Introduce the dog to as many adults, children and other dogs as possible in pleasant surroundings. This will make your Scottie more relaxed if you intend to show it, and it will also help the dog to be less aggressive to strangers who are visitors to your home.

Socialized or not, your Scottie will still kick up a terrible fuss if strangers lurk about the family property. It has a very protective instinct, and no knowledge of its size. Scotties are very verbal, and like to tell everybody off, except their owners and families. Mail carriers are scolded daily for messing with the family's mailbox. Trash collectors who come weekly to steal the family's great-smelling garbage are growled at, and barked away. Newspaper delivery people are told to stop throwing things at the front door, but like all service people, they don't listen! In no time at all, the Scottie is convinced constant vigilance is necessary to keep things safe at its home.

An over-zealous watchdog perhaps, but the Scottie means well. The dog serves its owner with loyalty and devotion for all of its life. Wherever you are is where this little dog wants to be. Some of you will feel the same way about your Scottie.

If, however, the Scottie is not what you're looking for, check out this shorthaired lovable pet.

PEMBROKE WELSH CORGI
Colors: Red, sable, fawn, black and tan with or without white.
Height: 10" – 12"
Weight: 25 – 30 lbs.

Beloved by the British royal family, the Pembroke Welsh Corgi has been a part of their family for decades. Queen Elizabeth owns several of them.

The breed's name comes from the Celt word for dog. Corgis came to Wales in the 12th century with Flemish weavers, and the Welsh used the dogs for herding cattle. The little dogs nipped the heels of straying animals to keep them in line.

A Corgi would rather play than fight, and usually adores children. Nevertheless, it's still a watchdog, and is protective of its territory. Strangers will be treated with suspicion. *Socialize* your pup at its special imprint time of twelve weeks. Introduce it to as many strangers and other dogs as possible in pleasant circumstances. This will help the dog to be more relaxed when strangers come to your home.

You would be a good owner for this one, Capricorn, because at times the dog gets over excited, stimulated by hyperactive people. Your matter-of-fact handling of the dog, and your loving heart will keep the dog on a steady course. You won't have to persevere with its training though. Corgis learn their lessons earlier than most breeds, and if you want to show it as a young dog, it will behave well in the ring.

You'll need to brush and comb your dog a couple of times a week to keep its coat in good condition.

The Pembroke has an inquisitive nature, and loves to explore its neighborhood, town or country. Walks are important for this sturdy, hardy little dog. Corgis love good food, and will beg tidbits from friendly munchers. Even though you are not usually indulgent, it's hard not to give in to its charming manner of begging. The Pembroke has such an appealing little face, and very expressive eyes. Being overweight is a serious problem for all dogs, but more so for dogs with short legs. If you are aware of this, you'll be stricter with its diet to keep the dog healthy – well most of the time anyway.

It would be difficult not to fall for a Pembroke once it becomes a part of your family. It's a charming little dog with one aim in life – to please you. For some of you, that would be a nice change.

The Pembroke has a cousin who is also a sweetheart – the **CARDIGAN WELSH CORGI**. It has a bushier tail, and bigger ears. Although similar in appearance, it is classified as a separate breed. The Celts brought the dog from Europe to Cardiganshire in Wales in the 12th century. Like the Pembroke, the dog was used on farms to herd cattle.

In temperament, the breed is less outgoing than its cousin, and is a quieter dog - less perky, but still ready for a game with a ball. If you want to show your dog, the Cardigan is very easy to prepare for the ring, and usually behaves well when traveling. It's a good breed for apartment living, but loves to go for a walk. There'll be no scrappy dogfights with this one as Cardigans behave with decorum.

The Pembroke is more popular on both sides of the Atlantic, but the Australians favor this loyal, faithful little dog. Check them both out. Either one will win your heart.

Finally, Capricorn, there are some spaniel breeds that are absolutely adored by their owners.

KING CHARLES SPANIEL
Colors: Black and White
Height: Up to 10"
Weight: 10 - 15lbs.

This aristocratic little spaniel has been a member of royal families for centuries. Van Dyck painted several portraits of King Charles with his spaniels in the 17th century. The dog was known as the Toy Spaniel, but it became the King Charles due to its favor with the king.

The variations of the King Charles are the **PRINCE CHARLES** (white with black and tan markings), the **RUBY** (chestnut red) and the **BLENHEIM** (white with red markings). A larger breed was developed in England from the Toy Spaniels and is known as the **CAVALIER KING CHARLES**. This popular spaniel can weigh up to 18 lbs., and is usually the color of the Ruby or the Blenheim.

The King Charles Spaniel is not temperamental. It's a steady, level-headed little dog; full of affection for its owner once a bond has formed. It doesn't like to be rushed into new experiences, and likes to take its time. At first you will find your pup shy, but once it gains confidence, and gets used to the home and family, it fits in nicely. If you own a cat, your King Charles will probably seek it out for a best friend.

The dog enjoys the outdoors. It's a hardy breed, but if the dog gets wet, it's important to towel it dry and make sure its bed is dry and clean. You should bathe its face after an outing outdoors. The little dog is inquisitive, and could get grit in its eyes. Check with your vet about ear care.

Grooming is an easy chore for the dog's coat just needs to be brushed weekly, with little or no trimming required. Exercise is needed daily to keep the dog fit. It loves its food, and will turn its liquid eyes on anyone in the family that's eating something that smells good. Indulgent owners cause the dog to become obese, but you are not likely to do this.

Sweet, affectionate and playful, Toy Spaniels are very special and it's not surprising that they roamed palaces for centuries, beloved by kings, and have now become very popular pets, adored in countless homes.

Pointers, Labradors, the Golden Retriever, the Kerry Blue, the Keeshond, the Scottie, Corgis, and King Charles Spaniels are the breeds we suggest for your sun sign personality, Capricorn. We hope we have been of help to you.

Good luck in picking your perfect pup

German Shorthaired
Pointers

LabradorRetriever

Golden Retriever

Kerry Blue Terrier

Keeshond

Scottish Terrier

Pembroke Welsh Corgi

Cardigan Welsh Corgi

King Charles Spaniels

AQUARIUS THE WATER BEARER
January 21 through February 19

Uranium is your metal
Your stone is an amethyst
Orchids are your flowers
And your color is an electric blue
Now let's find that pup compatible with you

Most of you would be generally concerned about the welfare of all breeds, and would be interested in knowing all about them. Learning about different breeds, and discussing them, does not mean you would actually want to own any of them. You are just curious folk. Before we get into the breeds that would be compatible with your personality, it's important to us that you understand where we're coming from.

Initially, as a professional astrologer and a canine behaviorist, our first question was, "What kind of dog owner would an Aquarius be?". We found the answer by thoroughly studying your sun sign personality. Once we knew what you would probably look for in a dog, we considered all of the breeds registered with the American Kennel Club to find some perfect pups for you. Now, we're not saying that you can only successfully own the dogs we have selected for you. What we are saying is that the pups we suggest would be good choices for your sun sign personality.

We'll first review the characteristics of your sun sign, and discuss dog traits and temperaments that could be a plus or a minus for you. Your compatible pups are then described in full so that you can make your own decision based upon your lifestyle and personal preference.

Your sign shows you to be the kind of person who supports noble causes and humanitarian issues. You are rarely prejudiced. Most of you believe in equality and the rights of all to live together in freedom.

Many of you are inventive and creative, interested in new ideas and would prefer to see things from an objective view most of the time. Philosophies intrigue you, and you don't need proof of ideas to be fascinated by them. Many of you are content to explore them as theories.

Emotions can get in the way of philosophical thinking. You prefer to remain detached

When your feelings are getting the better of you, most of you switch to mind over matter. You are really good at this. Your interests are so varied that it's easy for you, to turn off emotionally. Something unusual can be found to explore, or you'll become involved with a new project

Most of you resist conforming. You don't want to be told how to dress, behave, or how to spend your time. In fact, Aquarius, you dismiss most of the rules and regulations issued by others, especially if you see little need for them. You usually avoid anyone who tries to direct your life. Freedom to do your own thing, in your own way, is considered to be your right, and not a privilege.

If family members become too possessive, you balk, and resist the restriction forced on you. You're even surprised when they take it personally. You rarely see any reason for emotional scenes.

When you hear that a friend of yours has a problem unrelated to you, that's different. You're usually willing to do anything possible to help out. True, someone else will probably have to point it out to you, but once you are aware of it, you're there with bells on to do what you can.

People from all walks of life interest you. You can be as fascinated by a bag lady on the city streets as you are by meeting a celebrity. You don't discriminate on the basis of what people do, but are interested in what they have to say through their experiences.

There are times when you want to be left alone. Although you often enjoy being with a group of people, you'll sometimes remove yourself from the mainstream physically, mentally, or both. You probably won't let people know what you are thinking at these times. As outgoing and curious as you are when it comes to others, you are quite private when it comes to yourself. You'll usually share your ideas, but you won't share yourself too often.

Now, although you are expansive in your theories, philosophies, and the need for change in the world, this does not extend to the need to change yourself. Your own ideas and opinions remain as fixed as your right to have them, and keep them.

Some of you hold high positions of authority, but you do not usually exert power control over your staff, nor do you nurture them. You expect them to come though on their commitments as individuals who are part of your team. Following up on their work isn't a habit with most of you. In fact, following through on your own routine things would be a conscious effort for you. Although you can juggle several projects at one time, many of you may forget to complete the simple, everyday tasks expected of you.

It's generally understood in astrology, Aquarius, that the people who inhabit this planet will become more like you in the future. You are just ahead of your time. You're ruled by the planet Uranus, associated with the new and progressive ways of thinking in our world of today. Your traditional symbol of the Water Bearer means that you were born to pour the "Waters of Enlightenment" into the world. You are idealists, humanitarians, advanced thinkers, and innate philosophers. Perhaps you appear to be cold at times because you prefer not to be emotionally involved, but most of you seek ways to progress beyond the traditional bondages to create a free world of equality and human decency.

When it comes to owning a dog, most of you will be kind, but casual owners. It's not likely that you will seek a deep involvement with your canine buddy unless life has made you vulnerable, and you really need a friend. Some of you could be very fond of a mixed breed, respecting the dog for whatever it is without the need for a long line of pure ancestry. However, Aquarius, some breeds could give you problems, mixed or purebred. To help you to avoid taking such dogs under your wing, let's look at some plus and minus breed traits and temperaments for your Aquarian personality.

Breeds that require continuous, steady training are not a good idea. They would take up too much of your time, and routines, essential for such dogs, are not your usual style. In all honesty, you would probably forget you hadn't trained the pup since last Thursday, or was it the Thursday before?

Most you will be absolutely delighted to see the dog when you come home, and enjoy its welcome, but you're not likely spend a great deal of time with it. You'll probably have something else to do on your mind. Of course, the dog can tag along behind you if it wants to, but you'll actually leave this up to the dog. If the dog demands a lot of love and attention from you, misses you when you are gone, and becomes depressed by your long absences, you would be sympathetic in a general way, but probably decide that it's the dog that has the problem. It would be better for both you, and the dog, to get a breed that doesn't have a great need for your constant love and attention. A casually affectionate breed would suit you better.

Dominant, aggressive dogs would interest many of you. They are fine looking animals, and have lots of character. You wouldn't care for it if they tried to dominate you, though, and you are not too interested in dominating them. A dog that will not give you a challenge in this area would be a better choice for you.

You may have spurts of training your pup, but you'll have a tendency to let the dog develop naturally. It would be a good idea to choose a dog that comes with a natural instinct to protect you and your home. You will appreciate its enthusiastic protection on your behalf, and praise the dog to your friends.

A dog that does not invite your on-going interest could be absent-mindedly forgotten by some of you. Your dog should intrigue you, Aquarius. You'll enjoy talking about your canine buddy to your friends, and would prefer something startling to say about it. An interesting breed, with unusual character traits would please most of you.

If the dog was less than perfect, that would not be a problem for most of you. You rarely judge, and will often be fascinated by habits that would dismay other people. You'll accept its ways as part of who the dog is, and since it's your dog, you'll even see them in a positive light. You are very loyal to those you care about.

To sum up, Aquarius, your dog should not be a breed that needs to be consistently trained, nor should it be a dog that wants to dominate you. Most of you will not have the time or the understanding for a "clinging vine". You would appreciate a breed with natural protective instincts, and one that has lots of character.

The first breed recommended for you is not only unusual, it's also quite handsome.

CHOW CHOW
Colors: Red, black, cinnamon and cream
Height: 18"- 21"
Weight: 55 - 70 lbs.

Has owning a small bear ever appealed to you? The Chow Chow is the closest pet to it. Some authorities actually claim it has bear blood because of its profuse coat and blue-black tongue and mouth. It even has excellent balance when walking in rough terrain. Perhaps you may think that a Chow being a relative of the bear is only a wonderful theory, but there's fossil evidence that bears and dogs were once one animal, and has been considered by some authorities to be "the missing link".

The breed may have originated from the Tibetan Mastiff and the Samoyed, or possibly, the Norwegian Elkhound and Keeshond. It's all educated speculation, Aquarius, and you'll probably like the bear theory the best.

There are different theories also on why this handsome furry dog is called a Chow. Certainly the dog was food at one time, and its fur coat used for clothing. It's also suggested that its name comes from the days when these dogs were transported on sailing vessels, and were listed under the curios cargo – curios roughly translates to "chow-chow." Another authority claims its name comes from the Chinese word chaou, which means dog of great strength.

Protecting your property comes naturally to a Chow. It's thought that the Tartars brought this breed with them when they invaded China in the llth century B.C. Tartars, the fighting barbarians, used Chows to be their guard dogs and fighting companions.

The breed is non-intrusive, aloof and exceptionally independent. In fact, it's not only aloof to strangers, but could also be aloof to you if you do not make the necessary connection early, and bond with the dog. It's important that you *socialize* your pup at about twelve weeks old, which is its special imprint time. Introduce the pup to as many men, women, children, and wagging-tail happy dogs as possible. You probably know lots of people to show the pup off to, and this will help the dog to be more sociable and accepting of people who drop by. Of course, the Chow, even if well socialized, will still scowl at strangers, but it will accept them more easily.

As much as you like your space, Aquarius, you still want your dog to care about you, and Chows can be quite affectionate if their owners want it that way. Feeding and grooming the furry pup yourself helps. Since the mature dog has a very thick coat, regular brushing will be necessary. When you make brushing the pup a positive experience, with praise and a treat, your Chow will enjoy your attention and seek it from time to time.

There are two types of coats for Chows – rough and smooth. They both need brushing. Because their eyes are deep set, their peripheral vision is not great. Teaching the dog should be done face-to-face.

One of the things many of you will particularly like about the Chow is that the dog has retained its natural character. It has a proud and independent ancestry, and is used to taking care of itself. A Chow will rarely respond to anyone who shouts at it, or treats it harshly. It's a dog that chooses to amble beside you because it likes you. Chows are quiet companions in the home, gentle unless bullied. You won't be offended too often by a doggy smell for the dog is really clean in its habits.

This is a dog that can live just about anywhere, unless, of course, you live in a hot climate. A daily walk is important, but the dog doesn't need to be strenuously exercised.

Once a Chow has accepted you as its owner, the dog is very loyal. True, it might not choose to obey a command from time to time because it doesn't see the necessity for it, but the dog will act with intelligence and foresight when necessary. Your respect and general liking for unusual and special breeds, along with your kindness, is good for a Chow. Handled correctly, the dog will respond well to all family members, but will probably choose a favorite person as a pup.

Some Chow breeders do not recommend this dog for families with young children. It is not often tolerant of them.

Most of you are not likely to want to dominate your Chow, and it doesn't want to dominate you. If you make the effort when the dog is a pup, and form a bond with your small bear, you two will make a fine independent team for life.

If, however, you are looking for a country dog that absolutely loves the outdoors, check out this one.

BRIARD

Colors: Black, shades of gray, tawny shades
Height: 22"- 27"
Weight: 70 - 80 lbs.

The refined Chien Berger de la Brie, known to us as the Briard, was around in the 8th century, and was a multi-purpose dog. It was the official breed of the French army, and has been guarding sheep for centuries in its native France. As army dogs, they were favored by Napoleon, and were admired and loved by French soldiers. The dogs rescued wounded soldiers in battle, carried supplies and ran messages. As a sheepdog, the Briard is on guard day and night, ever alert and protective of the flock.

Most of you will particularly appreciate the Briard's quiet, attentive, intelligent nature, Aquarius, and the dog will warm quickly to your pleasant and friendly manner. This one would soon become timid if harshly trained for it's a docile breed. It's used to being alone, waiting quietly, but watchfully.

As an adult, the Briard is aloof to strangers. *Socialize* your pup at about twelve weeks, the special imprint time for all dogs, by introducing it to as many adults, children, and other dogs as possible in pleasant surroundings. Socialization will not affect its ability to be a good watchdog, but it will help the dog to be friendlier to your guests. Of course, if you intend to show your dog, socialization will help the dog to go for Best in a more relaxed manner. Since the breed has a steady temperament, it shows well, but if you want your Briard to be eligible for show, make sure your pup has the double dewclaw on its hind legs.

Training a Briard is not difficult once you have bonded with the pup. Since you'll need to brush its double coat of profuse hair at least once a week, you have an excellent way to bond. You are not a dominant person as a general rule, but brushing your dog's coat will remind the pup who was once in charge of grooming it, its mother, and will accept your lead role in its life.

It's a quiet dog. When it does bark, it will have good reason. It's not an active barker like a terrier is, but the dog listens and watches constantly for anything that may threaten you, your family or your home.

The country or the suburbs is a better home for the Briard. It loves to go for long walks. It usually enjoys a swim, but if you live by the ocean, be sure to wash off the salty water at the end of the day.

Your Briard will love you devotedly and loyally, Aquarius, and it will wait for you with incredible patience. Now that's something most of you will really appreciate since you do have a tendency to lose track of time when you are busy.

Perhaps, though, you would prefer a dog with less hair. If so, check out this unique breed.

SHAR-PEI

Colors: Rust, black, cream, dark fawn, white
Height: 16"-20"
Weight: 40 - 55lbs.

Just looking at a Shar-Pei pup will put a smile on your face, Aquarius. It looks like a pup wearing its mother's skin. We almost lost this breed. In 1979, the Guinness Book of World Records named it the world's rarest dog.

The breed dates back to the Han Dynasty (circa 220 A.D). The Chinese used them for mongoose hunters and farm dogs. Later on they were also put in the ring as fighting dogs, but they were not winners. They were far more suited to protecting their owners and their property.

When the Communists came to power in China they put a tax on pet dogs to stop food being wasted on them. This tax kept going up and by 1940 it was an uncommon sight to see a dog in China. In 1960 Shar-Peis were in danger of extinction. Matgo Law wrote to Dogs Magazine in the U.S., asked for help, and brought the danger of extinction of the breed to the notice of American breeders. In 1983 Neiman Marcus featured Shar-Peis in their Christmas catalogue. Nowadays, it's quite easy to purchase a Shar-Pei pup, but it's believed that a Boxer may have been added to the mix, as the breed was once listed as 165 lbs.

The dog is very clean. Some Shar Pei's clean themselves like cats. There's no shedding with this one either, Aquarius, as its coat is very short. It's not smooth, though. It has a bristle texture. Shar-Pei actually means sand-skin. The pup eventually grows into its skin, but not all the way. You'll find your adult dog has lots of wrinkles around its face and ears.

Although you will need to give this one some guidance, the dog is intelligent and learns quickly. Owners we spoke to told us that their dogs were housebroken without any help from them. That's a very nice plus.

Most of you will particularly like the way this dog stands, confident and calm, watching with alert, almond-shaped eyes. It trots beside you with an aristocratic air.

Another interesting thing to note about this breed is that its tongue and mouth are either blue-black or a shade of overall purple, depending upon the color of its coat. It's possible that Shar Pei's retained a little of its ancestry from the animal that roamed the earth centuries ago that was both bear and dog.

The dog is independent and full of dignity, Aquarius. Being submissive is not one of its traits. The mature dog is particularly aloof with strangers. It's important to *socialize* the pup at its special imprint time of twelve weeks. Introduce your interesting pup to as many strangers and other dogs as possible during this period to help it to be more comfortable when you have visitors, or if you want to show your Shar-Pei.

Your sun sign personality is good for this breed. You are kind and non-punitive. How close you are with your dog will depend on the bonding you make with the dog as a pup. Shar-Peis can be quite affectionate if encouraged by their owners. We think you will find the time to form the necessary connection – it's hard to resist spending quality time with such an adorable pup.

The next breed is for the Aquarius among you that want a stronger attachment with their dogs, and are looking for a constant companion.

BOXER
Colors: Fawn or brindle with white markings
Height: 21"- 25"
Weight: 55 -70 lbs

The Boxer we know today started in Munich, Germany in 1896. Opinions vary but it's thought to be descended from the Tibetan Mastiff, with some Bulldog and possibly Great Dane in its mix. The breed was first registered in America in 1904. The breed's climb to popularity was slow at first until people learned that the dog had a very sweet nature, and Boxers took top honors in the show ring.

Although the Boxer is a large dog, it's happy in an apartment, town house, country mansion, cottage, or suburban home. When trained, it's extremely well behaved. Boxers are responsible in the home, intelligent, and easily trained. They have become favored guide dogs for the blind. They are also K-9 recruits for the police and army. Boxers are known for being able to serve in whatever capacity required of them. They have an even temperament along with an inquisitive nature, keen mind and social graces.

Even when you are busy at home, Aquarius, you won't mind if your dog tags along. Your Boxer will follow you about. It's a breed that likes to be close to its owner. The dog will lie beside you quite happily, hoping to rest its head on your feet. There'll be times when it will drop its toy, probably a ball, at your feet, and stare fixedly at it until you toss it for retrieval.

Although your Boxer enjoys hanging out with friendly people, when you leave it at home alone, it will play happily for hours with its toys. Of course, you may find that old teddy bear you saved from childhood missing. Check your dog's bed. You'll probably find it stashed next to the green squeaky frog, rubber ball, one of your socks, and a rawhide strip.

If you have children, your Boxer will love them. Kids are wonderful playmates for a dog that, even when old and gray, always wants to play. *If you have cats, though, don't get a Boxer.* Some Boxers find a cat chase impossible to resist, delight in treeing felines, and will spend hours tracking them down in the home.

If you live where the winters are cold, you'll have to go shopping for sweaters for this one. Its coat is very fine and soft, and doesn't keep out the chill winds. Save your old towels, too. When your Boxer has been out in the rain, you should dry it off. If you live where the summers are hot, air conditioning is a must. Boxers shiver in the cold and pant in the heat.

Is it a guard dog? Opinions differ on this question, and it's possible that the dog behaves according to whether it feels an intruder intends bodily harm. Samantha—*see front cover*—alerts her owner to all passer-bys with low growls and barks. She's definitely a good watchdog.

Most Boxers do not respond well to total strangers, and are wary of them. *Socialize* your Boxer pup by taking it out to meet and greet people, and other dogs, at its special imprint time of three months. It would also be a good idea, Aquarius, if you did not get the pup when you plan to be away a lot. Your Boxer will choose its favorite person as a pup, so make sure you are a constant during its imprint time if you want that person to be you.

When people have had a Boxer as a member of the family, they rarely want any other breed. It's just that kind of dog. If you are looking for a smaller breed, however, particularly good for city apartments, check out this great American breed.

BOSTON TERRIER
Colors: Dark brindle with large white markings
Height: 15"- 17"
Weight: 15 – 25 lbs.

Although the Boston Terrier's ancestors were British and French, this breed is considered to be an American dog. The first known Boston Terrier was purchased by Robert Hooper of Boston. Boston breeders worked hard to get the breed recognized, and when they were successful, the dog became popular all over the U.S.

Although there are three sizes of Bostons, you should avoid getting too small a dog. Some of the very small ones have cranial problems. The fine original Boston was not a Toy.

It has been said that the Boston lacks intelligence because if it gets out of its yard, it has a problem finding its way home. This has nothing to do with the dog's intelligence. It has a very short nose, and has more trouble tracking than most breeds. If you take your pup for short walks around your neighborhood often, this should solve the problem.

Boston Terriers are lively, sweet companions with very good manners. In fact, in the 1930's they had the nickname of "The American Gentleman".

They are not aggressive, although they can hold their own if a larger breed attacks them. It's a kind dog, loyal and devoted to its family. Of course, with a bulldog in its mix, it can be stubborn. The dog has a live-and-let-live attitude, which most of you will understand totally. It doesn't want to be fussed over too much, nor does it respond to an owner who makes too many demands on its time. This dog thoroughly enjoys naptime, but it will be protective of its owner and of its home.

There's little grooming with a Boston, and its exercise needs are short walks. In your absence, the dog will settle happily until your return. It will probably choose to sleep in your favorite chair as it enjoys breathing in the scent of its owner. If you have a problem with this, you could try putting one of your old tee shirts in its bed. No promises on that one, though.

Your personality is good for this breed. The dog does not do well with a bossy owner. It will not make too many demands on your time, and will appreciate your casual expectations. Your Boston Terrier will respond to your kindness well, be a loyal friend, and live happily with you and your family in total harmony.

Now let's take a look at a dog which will interest all of you.

BASENJI
Colors: Black and white, fawn and white, tricolor
Height: 16"-17"
Weight: 22 - 24 lbs.

The Basenji is a dog that does not bark, but it has its own sound, which is not easy to describe. Perhaps a yodel is the closest description to its hound sound. Some authorities claim that this African Bush dog was taught not to bark when Basenji packs drove game into nets.

It's an ancient breed. Pictures resembling the Basenji were found on Egyptian rock carvings dating back 5,000 years ago. It's been called a terrier spitz breed, but falls under the category of the hound group. It wasn't until 1943 that the AKC officially recognized the breed.

Few know what a wonderful, sweet dog this is because a non-barking dog is an oddity. You, however, would find this very interesting and would not be put off by it. All those wrinkles on its forehead make people think that the dog is a worrier, but in the right hands, it's a happy little dog. A Basenji is very clean, and takes care of its grooming itself, much like a cat. It sheds a little, but a quick brushing will take care of loose hair.

The African tribesmen valued their hunting companions highly. They were treated with great respect, and encouraged to be spirited and independent. Today's Basenji has retained these traits. The dog is very wary of strangers, and should be *socialized* at its special imprint time of twelve weeks. Introduce your pup to strangers, and other dogs at this time to help the dog to be more comfortable when visitors come to your home.

Your Basenji will attach to you and to your family, but will not be fond of another dog in residence, especially if the other dog is brought in when the Basenji is an adult.

Basenji roughly translates to "jumping up and down dog" and it's true to its name. If you have a low fence in your yard, you may not find your dog there when you go to call it in.

The Basenji will not be over demanding of your time, but it does need to know you care. One of the ways this dog asks for affection is by sitting down, gazing at you with its almond-shaped dark eyes, rubbing its paw over its nose, and cocking its head to one side. Now who could resist that?

You won't have to worry about breakables with this dog's tail – it curls in a circle on its rump. Compact, agile, intelligent and independent, the Basenji is a delight. Some of you will thoroughly enjoy owning this one.

The next breed is a sensitive dog, needing a kind owner.

WHIPPET

Colors: Black, red, white, fawn or blue, also mixed coloring.
Height: 19"-22"
Weight: 25 - 45 lbs.

The Whippet is a sweetheart. It's a gentle dog, Aquarius, just right for those of you who are looking for a constant companion. The dog has charming manners, both in the home and outside, and will look to you for approval and love for all of its life.

The breed was developed in England. Whippet racing was a very popular sport in the 19th century. Whippets were also bred for hunting game by sight. They coursed game at high speeds. It was the English mill operators who brought the dog to the U.S. and the AKC recognized it in 1888.

Greyhounds, Italian Greyhounds, Manchester Terriers, Airedales and English terriers are said to be in the mix, but authorities differ. They also differ on why the whippet is known as the snap-dog. One authority claims that when dogs met on a straight course, they snapped at each other. Another claims that it is because the dog can change its direction without slowing down.

It's an easy dog to keep clean, Aquarius. Its coat is short, soft and silky to the touch, and its little feet leaves small prints. Groom your dog to calm it, and to keep its coat shiny and clean. It's a good idea to rub the dog down with a piece of chamois leather.

The dog is very quiet in the home, but when outside, make sure you have a fenced yard. This dog can be gone in a matter of seconds if a rabbit happens by. The dog is usually good at playing catch, and at agility games. If you live in the city, in an apartment, that's fine so long as you walk the dog, and if you have interest in seeing the dog run, it can do so by entering the dog into Whippet races, or Lure Coursing. Whippets also show well.

Socialize this sweet pup when its three months old by introducing it to as many friendly adults, children, and dogs as possible in pleasant surroundings. This will help to calm the dog when strangers are about, but it is not a watchdog, and is usually friendly to visitors unless they are loud and boisterous people.

It's easy to train a Whippet. You won't even have to raise your voice, but it's important to remember that Whippets grow out of their puppy stages slowly, and do not mature until well into their second year. Pushing a Whippet is not wise. The dog is usually submissive to its owner. Anyone who shouts a lot at a Whippet will have trouble finding the dog. It will hide away.

Since most of you avoid violence in any form, and prefer a peaceful home, a Whippet should be happy with you. This gentle dog is so sweet and responsive it's often used as a therapy dog for the aged and infirm who need a friend.

If you live where winters are cold, you'll need a coat for your dog, and it should always be housed inside. As your vet will advise, careful use of anesthesia is important, and some Whippets have an irregular heart beat when at rest. This is said to be common for a Whippet, and the dog has a regular heartbeat when exercised.

The next breed we suggest is a mischievous little dog, that will put a grin on many of your faces.

DACHSHUNDS – SMOOTH, WIRE, LONGHAIRED
Colors: Red, fawn, speckled with black, black and tan.
Height: 5"- 9"
Weight: 23 – 25 lbs.
Miniature size is less than 10 lbs.

Dachshund means badger dog in German. This dog has also been known as the Teckle. They have been around for centuries – drawings of them seen in the 15th century. Dachshunds were used to flush badgers from their holes as well as rabbits, hares and foxes. Fearless, and bold, it dashes into the thickest covert, and wriggles down incredibly narrow burrows to reach its prey. Rats or moles don't have a chance if there's a Dachsi about.

You have three choices when choosing a Dachshund pup, Aquarius. The smoothhair variety is the most common. The wirehaired variety was possibly obtained by crossing the smooth with a Griffon, and then a Dandie Dinmont, which would explain its bushy beard and eyebrows. To obtain the longhair variety, smooths were probably bred with spaniels.

All of the varieties of this breed are intelligent, independent, and totally lovable, but they do differ somewhat in personality. The smooth Dachshund tends to be more outgoing than the more reserved, gentler, long-haired Dachshund. The wirehair breed is sportier, with terrier behavior.

All three types will respond very well to your personality, Aquarius. Aggressive owners who make lots of demands will have problems with Dachshunds. Independent, they resist abject obedience. They are usually very busy dogs, and if they are not guarding your home with total dedication, they are checking out the yard for vermin.

The smoothhaired Dachshund needs little grooming. The longhaired will need regular brushing to stop tangles from forming in its coat – they can really hurt. Brushing once a week should do it. The wirehaired will need more care in that its facial hair should be combed regularly, and it will need to be taken to a professional for plucking twice a year.

Dachshunds are affectionate. From time to time they stop dashing about, lie on their backs, wave their paws in the air, begging for a belly scratch. Briefly, they look submissive, but don't let this fool you. Your dog will live with you, love you, beg with expressive eyes, but it will always be focused on its own activities. When you give your dog a command, there won't even be a hesitation in the dog's mad dash away from you and your words. It's probably on a mission, and has very important things to do. Most of you won't take it personally, but treats work the best in getting your Dachshund's attention – the little dog usually has time to stop for a snack.

Dachshunds have been called hot dogs, sausage dogs, and wieners. They wouldn't care for their nicknames. They are proud little dogs, and can be even dignified. You'll grin down at your little friend, responding to its intelligent, mischievous eyes, and then go off to do your own thing. You'd better check on what your dog is up to. The lady next door might not know there's a mole in a hole amongst her prize shrubs.

The Chow, Briard, Shar-Pei, Boxer, Boston Terrier, Basenji, Whippet, and Dachshunds are the breeds we suggest for your sun sign personality, Aquarius. We hope we have been of help to you.

Good luck in picking your perfect pup.

Chow Chow

Briard

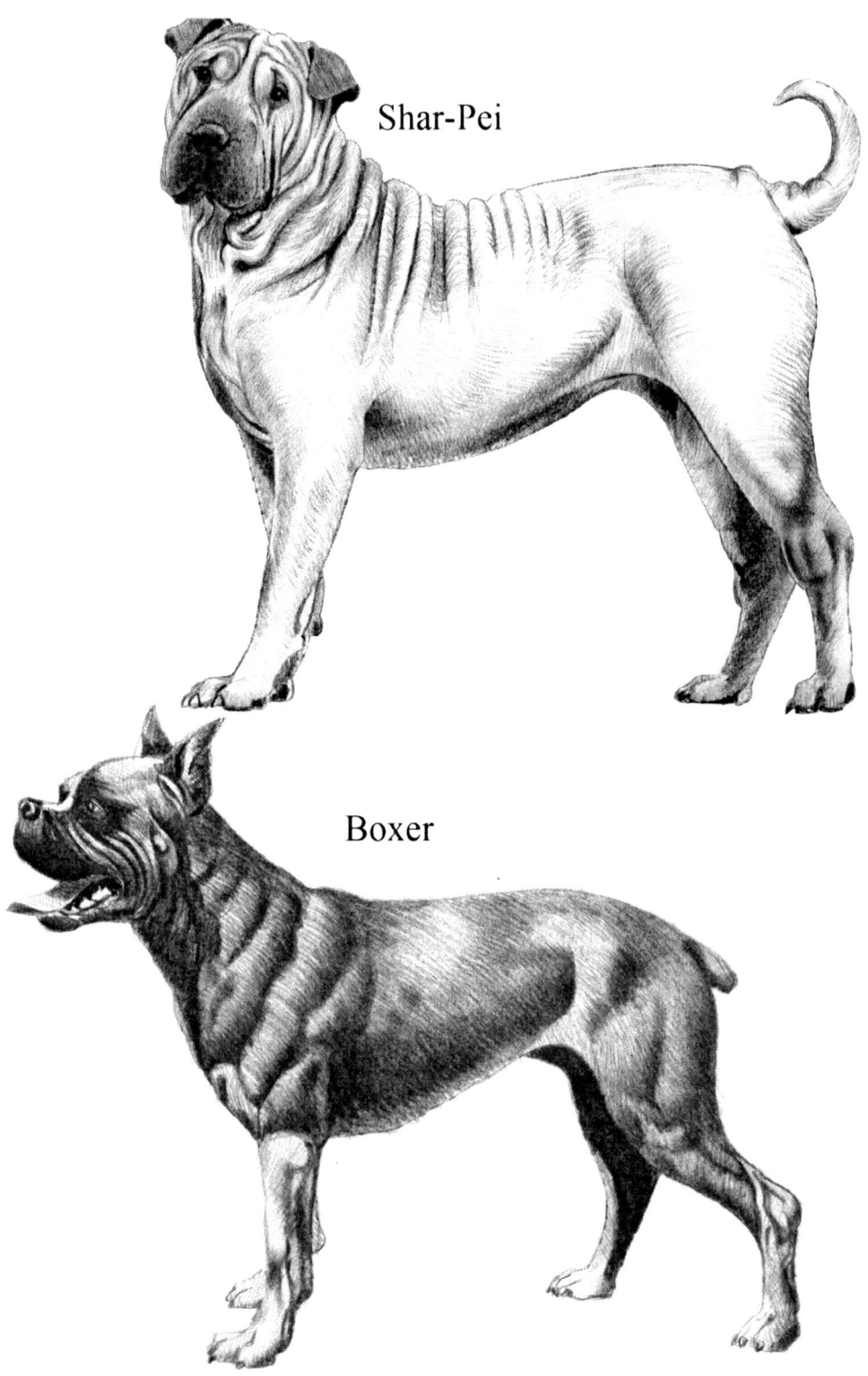

Shar-Pei

Boxer

Boston Terrier

Basenji

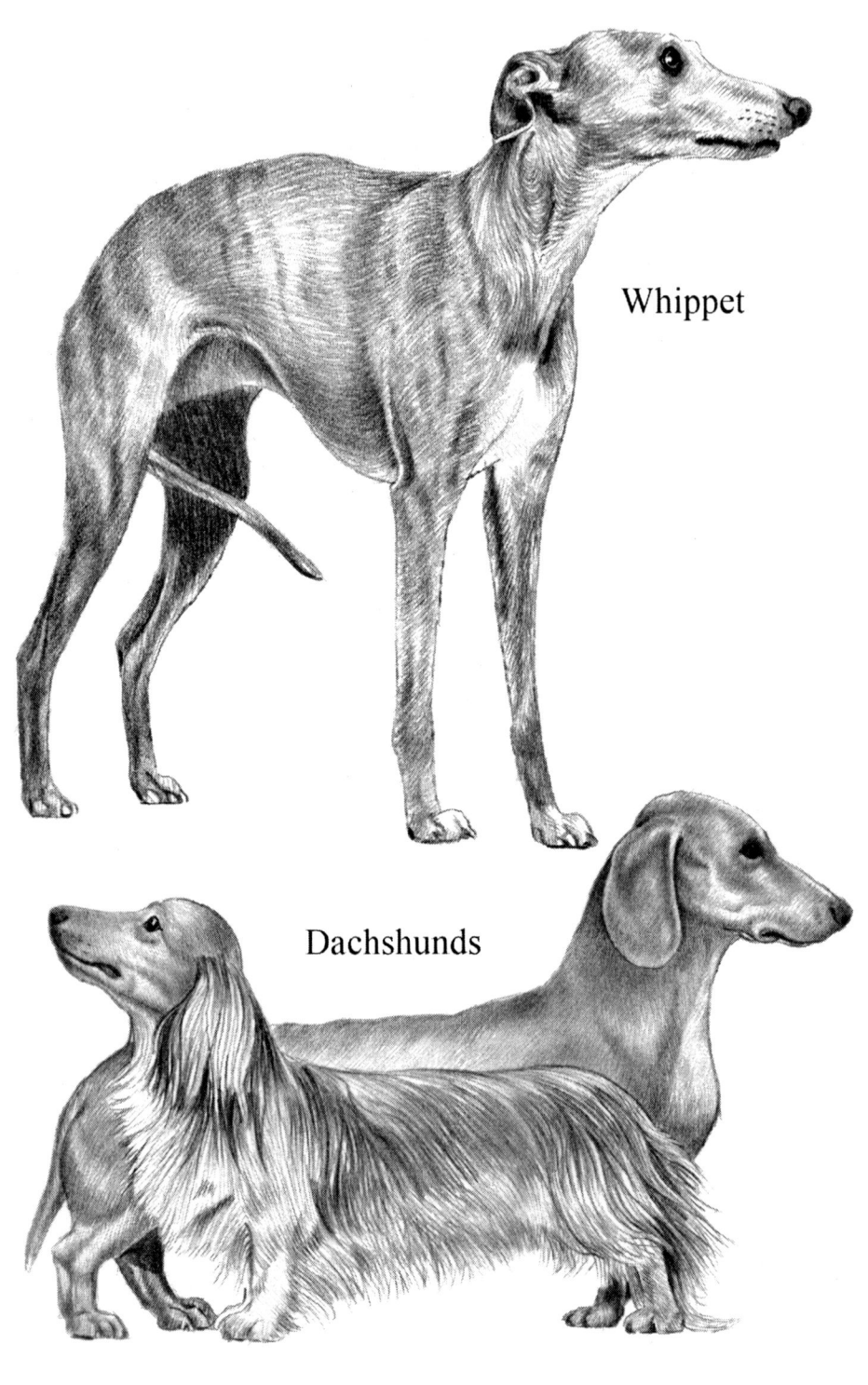

Whippet

Dachshunds

PISCES THE FISH
February 20 through March 20

Tin is your metal
Your stone is moonstone
Water lily is your flower
And your color is the blue green of the sea
You need a pup that suits you emotionally

You are the sensitive, gentle people of the zodiac, and most of you are concerned about the welfare of all dogs. Your heart would go out to a sad little mutt running about the streets looking for shelter and someone to care. Many of you would even put your life on hold to find the help the dog needs. But let's consider your needs, Pisces. Although compassion for the unwanted is a part of you, the right dog for your personality would bring joy into your life. Before we get into discussing which dogs could do this for you, though, it's important to us that you understand where we're coming from.

Initially, as a professional astrologer and a canine behaviorist, our first question was, "What kind of dog owner would a Pisces be?". We found the answer by thoroughly studying your sun sign personality. Once we knew what you would probably look for in a dog, we considered all of the breeds registered with the American Kennel Club to find some perfect pups for you. Now, we're not saying that you can only successfully own the dogs we have selected for you. What we are saying is that the pups we suggest would be good choices for your sun sign personality.

We'll first review the characteristics of your sun sign, and discuss dog traits and temperaments that could be a plus or a minus for you. Your compatible pups are then described in full so that you can make your own decision based upon your lifestyle and personal preference.

Your sign shows you to be an extremely emotional person. You are very intuitive and often act on hunches.

Your moods change often. Some of you can be light hearted, quiet, in tears, or angry in a matter of hours. Moving in and out of emotions can totally exhaust you. The wise ones amongst you will seek some alone time regularly to revitalize yourselves.

Unfortunately, a brief time out will not always be enough recuperation for you. A gentle soul, you are sometimes abused by others or by the harsh realities of life. When you try too hard, you feel as though you are being pulled into a whirlpool, and going under for the third time. Escape is imperative. If there's a chance to get away from it all to the mountains, the country, the beach or to visit a friend in another town, you'll grab it. While away, you can get a better perspective on what's happening in your life, and find the inner strength to cope.

If you can't physically remove yourself from your stress, some of you will tune out through music, and tune in to your dreams. You have wonderfully creative imaginations, and not many can weave dreams like a Pisces.

Sometimes your inner stress has little to do with your own life. You are a friendly and sympathetic person, and are often popular. People are instinctively drawn to you, and want to share their personal lives with you. A sob story is sure to catch and hold your attention. You are compassionate, and will often take on the sadness of another, empathetic enough to feel it as though it was happening to you. You care, Pisces, sometimes too much for your own good.

However, it is this feeling of empathy that's responsible for many of you being fine dramatic actors. When you take a role in a play or a film, you actually become the character. Finding yourself again when you have played your final scene, though, is not easy. From birth, you do not feel as though you have a definite shape.

Most of you need to be involved in something creative. If you do not seek the theater as an outlet for your creativity, you'll paint, write or design. Some of you can create things of incredible beauty because you transfer your depth of feeling into your work. The right outlet for your talents can be a problem. Vague apprehensions from within tend to stem your confidence in yourself. Some of you drift through life, absorbing it through all of your senses, but are unable to focus.

One of your weapons against life's handouts is humor. At times you have a clever tongue. When hurt, you can also use that tongue of yours to lash out at the offender with a cruel, cold remark or with a trade of angry words. Pushed too far, you may go within, and become indifferent.

Most of you are eager to learn about new concepts. You are particularly interested in becoming involved with projects that will help mankind. You want to contribute to important changes – to help others. Your paycheck would not be sufficient reward for working. You need to feel you are doing something of worth to feel of worth yourself.

Most of you have high ideals. You don't want to attack, lead, or control. Of more importance to you is inner peace.

You are an old soul, Pisces, and are wise. You were born with an understanding heart. Some of you have a sixth sense which keeps you and your loved ones safe from harm.

Your sign, Pisces, is two fish swimming in opposite directions. This symbolizes the fluctuation of your emotions that pull you in different directions. It also symbolizes the duality of your personality. Although you live in the real world physically, your mind and emotions seek the realm of fantasy.

The characteristics of your sun sign show that you will probably fall for your pup on its first day with you. All pups are sweet, and you have a heart that's ready and willing to be won over. Seconds after the pup has covered you with doggy sniffs and kisses, you're in love. If the pup does not grow up to be compatible with you, then you have a problem. Most of you would find it impossible to make your own dog one of the unwanted. This is a dilemma we want to help you to avoid, Pisces. Let's now look at some aspects of dog owning you probably wouldn't appreciate, and explore breed traits and temperaments that would be a negative or a plus for you.

Most of you are not looking for a power struggle. Breeds which demand a firm hand with an Alpha to lead them would not be compatible with your personality. These dogs' dominance challenges would be tiresome for you. You don't need this kind of hassle. A pup that will respond to you because you are its loving owner would be your kind of dog.

There will be days when you'll come home exhausted, just able to let the dog out or give it a quick walk before you relax. If you have a restless dog that demands much more from you, your patience will be sorely tried. Since you are a considerate person, you could feel uncomfortable in not being able to cope with the dog's demands. A calm, quiet breed in the home would be more in tune with your needs.

Now, although you don't want a dominant breed or a restless, demanding one, you do want one that will run and play with you in the sunshine or in the rain. In fact, Pisces, such a dog could uplift your spirits by sharing in your fun times. When you feel the joys of life, you will want to share them with your dog. Together you will run across the beach, tramp though the woods, or enjoy a stroll in a city park.

Some of you will seek your dog as a source of affection. You need to be loved by someone all of your life, Pisces, and if things are not going well in your personal life, you'll probably sit on the floor and hug your dog. If you owned a breed that didn't hug you back, or at least give you a kind look, you would definitely feel worse. You would be much happier with a cuddly friend to hug – an affectionate dog.

A highly-strung breed is also not a good idea for many of you.

Certainly they can be very affectionate, even doting, and would be there for you when you needed them. However, most of you change your moods more often than your socks, and this could be somewhat confusing for a dog with an anxious temperament.

Well, so far we have eliminated the aggressive, dominant breeds, restless dogs that demand too much attention, distant breeds, and those with a nervous temperament. Dogs with a calm, but playful nature, able to return your affection, and to be responsive and accepting of all your moods would be good breeds for you.

Finally, Pisces, you want a dog that will learn to obey you through its devotion for you. You will train the pup with love and kindness. Punishment for misbehavior will usually be mild. Your dog should want to please you, and try its best not to disappoint you in any way. Most of you should get a dog that needs you as much as you need the dog.

Give some thought to your lifestyle as you browse through the breeds we have suggested for you.

The first breed is very popular for all of the right reasons.

GOLDEN RETRIEVER
Colors: Pale cream to gold
Height: 21.5" - 24"
Weight: 60 - 75 lbs.

Some authorities claim that the Golden is a cross between Russian Sheepdogs and British Bloodhounds, and one story claims that Lord Tweedmouth, an English breeder who owned an estate on the Tweed River, purchased eight Russian sheepdogs in the mid 1800's. He bred them with bloodhounds to increase their scenting ability, and produced the Golden we know today. Another authority believes that Lord Tweedmouth, mixed the local Tweed Yellow Water Spaniel with an Irish Setter and English Bloodhound to achieve the Golden Retriever.

However this breed was achieved, the Golden Retriever is a beautiful dog with an intelligent, obedient, loyal and faithful nature. It's easy to train, and once the dog has been trained, it rarely forgets to stay on task. The Golden is a winner in Obedience, at Field Trials, as a guide dog for the blind, as an assist dog for the disabled, as a search and rescue dog, and in many other fields.

It's an excellent sporting breed, retrieving tirelessly from land or water regardless of weather conditions.

Although the dog works reliably in the worst of weathers, it's not good at weathering harsh treatment. A Golden has a sensitive nature and an overwhelming need to please its owner. It will certainly stay out of your way if you are not in a good mood. When it needs to bother you, the dog will gently paw your knee to attract your attention.

This dog is exceptionally popular, Pisces because of its amiable temperament. It loves children, and is an excellent housedog. Why we think it would be a good dog for you is because this is a dog that needs an owner who truly needs the dog. When neglected, and not given enough love and attention, the dog can go off its food and droop in spirit.

You'll need to brush your dog's longhaired coat often as it sheds. It's a good idea to start grooming your Golden when it's a pup. Make it a pleasant experience. The Golden loves to be brushed by a loving hand, and the bond between you will grow quickly. Apollo, a Golden in our family, loved being sung to, so if you like to sing, Pisces, play music softly, and sing a song to your pup as you groom.

This breed can be left at home alone, but be prepared for a big welcome and a present when you come home. Your dog will grab the nearest thing at hand to give you. The trait is instilled from when hunters praised the dog for retrieving downed quail. If you don't want a closet filled with odd shoes, try keeping some of the dog's toys close to the front and back doors of your home.

Although the Golden is not an aggressive dog, it's still wise to *socialize* it at its special imprint time of twelve weeks by introducing it to as many strangers and other dogs as possible. Socialization will help your dog to be more comfortable in your absences in the care of strangers, and to be more confident in strange places for all of its life.

It really doesn't matter where you live if you own a Golden. The dog adapts to country, town and city life. It loves a romp on the beach, or in the woods. Exercise is important as it's a sporting breed, and it absolutely loves to go for walks. If you live near the ocean, and the dog plays in the salt water, be sure to hose off the salt at the end of the day to avoid dermatitis. Your Golden will love to travel with you by car also, and is up for anything you have in mind. Once your dog attaches to you, it wants to be wherever you are.

Few dogs can offer you the depth of devotion of a Golden, Pisces, and many of you will fall forever in love with this multi-purpose, talented dog. However, the next breed is also special in its own way.

ENGLISH SETTER
Colors: White with black, lemon, orange and blue markings
Height: 21"- 26"
Weight: 60 - 70lbs.

Although this breed is named the English Setter, the breed is thought to have had its beginnings in France when breeders crossed a Spanish Pointer with a French Pointer. In the early 1800's, the breed was brought to Britain, and was developed by the renowned breeder Edward Laverack. It's possible that the Water Spaniel and the Springer Spaniel were then added to the mix.

English Setters were first shown in Britain in 1859, and were brought to the U.S. a few years later, where the breed gained a loyal following.

The city is not an ideal environment for this sporting breed. It loves to scent the earth, and explore the woods and fields. In safe areas, you can release the dog once it has learned recall.

If you feel strongly about the birds in your backyard, set up feeders for them, and enjoy watching them, this breed is not for you. English and American hunters have trained the dog to stalk and set birds for hundreds of years. It would be impossible to retrain the dog to ignore birds in its own backyard. Of course, the dog is not likely to catch them, but the birds might start to build their nests elsewhere.

A well-groomed English Setter is both elegant and beautiful, Pisces. You'll love to stroke its silky coat. Start grooming the pup as soon as it has settled into your home. It will really help to cement the bonding between you, and will be a pleasant experience for both of you.

Although this dog will become fond of all of the family members, it tends to give its devotion to one special person. This will be the person who feeds it, walks it, grooms it and trains it. The dog is capable of great trust and loyalty, Pisces, and will return your affection in full measure.

Your kindness and intuitive understanding is needed for this one's puppy stages. *One of its breed traits is that it's slow to mature.* Harsh criticism as a pup will make the dog unsure of itself, and it could lose its confidence. This pup is eager to please you, Pisces, and will learn its lessons, but it just needs you to be patient.

Treats work well with an English Setter, but treats could also be its downfall. It loves people food, and begs with very expressive hazel eyes. One thing an English should not be is fat.

When the young English Setter is happy, it is very playful. It's a family dog, but you'll need to keep a watchful eye if you have tots or the dog could knock them down in its eagerness to show them affection.

Exercise is important for this energetic breed, but it can match Houdini on its escape feats. Make sure you have a fenced yard, and check for a tunnel in progress. Escape is something you know all about, Pisces, but forewarned is forearmed when it comes to your English Setter.

A silky coated English Setter is full of sweetness, but if it's a large furry dog that you are looking for, check out this one.

SAMOYED

Color: White
Height: 19"- 23.5"
Weight: 50 - 65 lbs.

The Samoyede tribes were nomads in the Arctic regions, mainly in northeast Siberia, and their sled dog is named after them. In 1889 Robert Scott, the British explorer, was so impressed with these beautiful furry dogs that he brought some home with him to England. This was when Samoyeds' coats were black, and black and white, in addition to pure white. English breeders concentrated on the white to produce a truly spectacular show dog. When the dogs were introduced to Americans they were also favored for Show. In time the dogs' true calling was discovered – being harnessed to sleds for racing.

The very first dog to walk on the South Pole was a Samoyed, part of the expedition led by Roald Amundsen in 1911. Britain's Queen Alexandra really favored this spitz breed.

For centuries the dog has been a sled dog, living with other dogs, hunting, herding reindeer, and protecting members of the tribe. It's a live-and-let-live canine, Pisces. It is neither hostile to strangers nor aggressive to other dogs.

One thing that really bothers a Samoyed, though, is hot weather. *If you live in a hot climate, it would be unkind to get a Samoyed.* It has a double, dense coat. If you live in a climate where winters are snow filled and very cold, you'll have a happy Samoyed.

One of the reasons that this dog would be good for you, Pisces, is that you will understand the dog's needs. As a pup it is slow to gain bladder control. This is a genetic trait and has nothing to do with the dog's intelligence. Samoyeds are bright and alert. Members of the breed have scored highly in Obedience, and their companionable nature makes them good therapy dogs.

The dog is loyal to its own family members, but if you want it to be friendly with visitors, *socialize* the pup at twelve weeks by taking it out to meet and be petted by strangers. The moment you step out of your door with a Samoyed pup on a leash, people will be delighted to meet the pup. It's absolutely adorable.

Although constant bathing is not necessary for this one, regular combing and brushing is important. Grooming your Samoyed is a wonderful way to bond with your dog. Like all spitz breeds, it is up to the owner as to how attached the dog will be. If handled in the right way, a Samoyed pup will grow up to be a gentle, loyal, affectionate, protective companion. It's said that the constant reliance on man for survival has made the dog very intuitive to its owner's needs. When you need your space, your Samoyed will give it to you, and when you call, it will come with a grin on its face.

The next breed is for the Pisces among you who want to hang out with a gentle giant.

BERNESE MOUNTAIN DOG
Colors: Black with brown patches, white chest, sometimes - white mask
Height: 25" - 32"
Weight: 90 - 125 lbs.

The Bernese Mountain dog is Swiss, and it's thought that they first came to Switzerland with the Roman Legions, and fought alongside them in battle. Later they were used to pull carts for cheese makers and weavers, and as guardians of herds in the mountains.

When their need as working dogs went into decline, a breeder in Berne set out to save the breed. The dog became known for its willingness to obey its owner, and for its good manners in the home.

Although the Bernese is an excellent guard dog, it is not aggressive generally. You'll see these dogs pulling cartloads of laughing Swiss children at fairs or shows. The Bernese likes children, and is amazingly tolerant of them.

The dog has a long, soft and silky coat with a tendency to curl, especially on its rump. You'll need to groom the dog regularly, but as with all breeds, this is an excellent way to bond with your dog. If you prefer a smooth coat, then there is a smooth variety of this breed. Both have almond-shaped brown eyes.

Socialize the pup at twelve weeks, the special imprint time for all dogs, to make it easier on the dog when you have to kennel it, or put it into someone else's care for a while. This will not change its protective instincts.

A practical note is that a dog of this size needs a lot of dog food, and could affect your budget, but if you can afford to own this one, it's well worth the expense. An additional lifestyle consideration is where you live. Hot climates are not advised for a Bernese Mountain dog.

The next breed is the most popular dog on both sides of the Atlantic, and one which most of you would definitely add to your list of best friends.

LABRADOR RETRIEVER
Colors: Black, chocolate, yellow
Height: 21" - 24"
Weight: 55 - 80 lbs.

It's not surprising that Labs are one of the most popular dogs in the U.S. It's truly an exceptional breed. As a pup it will strive to please you, Pisces, and you will soon become very attached. It's highly intelligent, easily trained, and capable of great devotion.

The breed originally came from Newfoundland, was refined in Labrador, and enthusiastically adopted by the British. It's an excellent hunting dog, good in the field and in water. Labs are literally tireless, and ignore bad weather conditions. If you intend to hunt, you'll find this dog very responsive to learning the rules. The dog's obvious love of the sport, and the outdoors, makes it an ideal hunter's companion.

Because it was originally bred to be a hunting dog, and praised when it retrieved its quarry, your Lab will bring you a present the moment you enter the house, even if you just went out to get the mail. Tika, a Chocolate Lab in our family, usually grabs a shoe as her welcome gift, and if your Lab chooses to do the same, it's hard to match up a pair on a busy morning. It's a good idea to keep a few of the dog's toys close to the front and back doors.

There is a difference in the colors of the breed in our opinion. Black Labs have a more mellow temperament. Yellow labs are beautiful, but need firmer handling, and Chocolate Labs are usually more highly strung. You would be a good owner for all the colors of this breed, Pisces, because of your sympathetic nature and understanding of the pup's sincere efforts to work with you. The bond will grow quickly between you, and your pup will scamper after you wherever you go. This pup has a need to attach, and it will develop well with an affectionate and companionable owner.

Labs get along with children very well, and usually like most adults. However, they can be quite choosy about visiting dogs. *Socialize* the pup at its special imprint time of twelve weeks with as many friendly people and canines as you can find. It will help the dog to be more relaxed in crowds, and in strange surroundings. If you intend to show the dog, this is especially important. Labradors have taken Best in Show on both sides of the Atlantic.

Exercise is important and your Lab will quiver with excitement when you hold up its leash. The dog loves to go for walks, and enjoys the woods, parks and beaches. When the dog has learned recall, you can take off its leash in a safe area without concern. If you live by the ocean, though, it's important to hose off the salt on the dog's coat to avoid dermatitis.

It's not a good idea to leave your Labrador alone for long periods. If a Lab is denied human companionship it can become quite depressed. This is not likely to happen with you, though, Pisces. You will be intuitive where your canine friend is concerned.

Labradors are wonderful dogs, but if you are looking for a companion dog to simply hang with you, check out the armchair clown.

BASSET HOUND

Colors: Black/white/tan, red/white, pale tan/white
Height: 13"- 15"
Weight: 44 - 51 lbs.

A Basset pup will totally charm you, Pisces. At first, it can't find its center of balance. Its body is too big for its legs, and as the pup scampers across the floor, it falls over itself. Check that the baby gate is across the stairs. Tumbles are frequent with a Basset pup.

Much like the larger breeds, a Basset grows out of its puppy stages slowly. It will need your kind heart to do well. An easy-going owner is best for this one, because if you were to demand too much, too soon, the pup could become stubborn. It's not a breed prone to instant and quick obedience. In fact, the dog likes to mull over its options. However, once your pup has attached, it obeys through its devotion – well, most of the time.

A Basset in the home is a quiet, lazy hound. It loves to take a nap at any hour of the day or night. Rustle its treat box, or open the refrigerator door, though, and the snoozing hound you left in another room is by your side in a flash.

Use doggie treats when training, and for obedience. It's amazing how bright your Basset will become when there's something delicious in your pocket. However, too many snacks will make a Basset fat, and a fat Basset is not a wholesome sight. The dog waddles about on its little legs, trying to keep its tum off the floor. Since you will be primarily concerned about the health of your dog, most of you will not be over-indulgent with people food.

The Basset does have another interest, and that's going for a walk. Once outside, your sleepy Basset changes its personality. It becomes a hunting dog, and energetically explores the woods and the fields. The French bred this dog as a badger hound, and if there's a badger within a five-mile radius, your Basset will let you know with its hound sound. If any of you are interested in seeing what a Basset can do, you can observe them at the Basset Hound Field Trials. Perhaps you may like to train and enter your own Basset.

A Basset also shows well, and has taken top honors at shows on both sides of the Atlantic.

Grooming this one is an easy chore. A Basset has a soft, silky, short-hair coat. It will love to be brushed by you, and it will soak up your attention and affection. When you are not home, your Basset will curl up in your favorite chair, as it loves to breathe in your scent when napping in your absence.

Without a doubt, these dogs are con artists, which is why they are affectionately nicknamed "armchair clowns". When the dog doesn't want to do something, it tries several ways to get out of it. It could develop sudden deafness, affect a limp, or lie prone at your feet. Before you call the vet, rattle the dog's treat box. Some of you will understand this dog very well, and know what it's up to. You will respond to the dog's definite character traits and undeniable charm. Most of you will find it hard to resist the soulful look of a Basset Hound.

For the Pisces, who are looking for a small, lovable companion, we have Toy breeds to suggest to you.

POMERANIAN
Colors: White, red, orange, black or gray
Height: 10"- 11"
Weight: 4 - 6 lbs.

This little dog's courage, intelligence and sense of pride have little to do with its size. When being shown, it has a delightful arrogance, and has been known to trot off with Best, even for obedience. Queen Victoria often nodded her head in approval at how well her favorites were doing. The Queen bred Poms for show, and it is largely due to her interest in the breed that they became so popular.

Pomeranians come from Pomerania, which is south of the Baltic Sea, and is now recognized as part of Germany. It was once a sheepherder, weighing about 30 lbs., but over the years, the dog has been bred down to Toy size. Although the dog was first shown in America in 1892, the AKC didn't recognize the breed until 1900.

It's a miniature spitz breed with a double, profuse coat. Its feathery tail curls over its back and touches its neck ruff. You will love its bright, dark eyes, Pisces, which will gaze into yours with unconditional trust.

A Pom is super protective of its owner, and tends to overreact to what the dog decides is a threat. It protects you with fierce yaps. You should *socialize* this small dog when it is twelve weeks old, the special imprint time for all breeds. Introduce the dog to strangers, adults, and children, in pleasant circumstances, but take care they don't hurt the pup or the whole purpose of the exercise would be lost.

Poms are friendly, outgoing little dogs when treated well, and you'll make sure your Pom is treated with respect and kindness. Its coat will need brushing and combing a couple of times a week to keep it tangle free. Tangles hurt, and tend to put the Pom off from being petted, even by you. The dog loves to be groomed by a gentle hand. It seems to know it looks absolutely beautiful. When the grooming is complete, there's an extra spring in the dog's step as it trots up to other family members to show off and receive praise and a treat.

Another Toy breed, which may be of interest to you, Pisces, is also very popular because it's a sweetheart.

MALTESE
Colors: Pure white, pale ivory
Height: 8" - 10"
Weight: 6.5 - 9 lbs

The Maltese is an ancient breed from the island of Malta. Some authorities believe it originated in Melita, Asia Minor, and was once called Melitenia. This was around the first century BC. Aristocratic Romans and Greeks thought very highly of the breed, and treated the dog like royalty. Certainly, it has been revered for centuries, and is depicted on Greek artifacts and paintings. The AKC recognized the breed in 1888.

It is out of the question to treat a Maltese with unkind or harsh treatment, which is why you would be a good owner for this pup. A Maltese attaches to its owner with great loyalty and affection. It's a bright, happy little dog that loves to romp and play, and is much hardier than it looks. Your Maltese would love to scamper beside you on long walks.

The dog is intelligent, and is not difficult to train as it wants to earn your approval. However, you should try to forget how little it is, and treat it as though it were a much larger breed. A pampered and spoilt Maltese tends to be over-possessive, and loses much of its potential if smothered with love.

Socialize the dog at twelve weeks, the special imprint time for all breeds, so it is better able to share you, Pisces. Introduce the beautiful pup to as many strangers as possible in pleasant circumstances, but make sure your pup has been brushed well. Strangers petting the Maltese who has tangles in its coat will defeat the purpose of socialization.

The dog will need grooming daily, and will need its face washed. If you intend to show your Maltese, a professional is advised. The dog loves being shown, and trots around the ring with confidence and pride.

The pup should be encouraged to sleep in its own little bed with its own toys. It would prefer to sleep with you, of course, but if you permit this, you will be encouraging the possessive trait of the dog, and will not be able to share your bed with another if you so choose.

Many of you will fall in love with your Maltese.

Golden Retrievers, English Setters, Samoyeds, Bernese Mountain Dogs, Labradors, Basset Hounds, Pomeranians, and the Maltese are the breeds we suggest for your sun sign personality, Pisces. We hope we have been of help to you.

Good luck in picking your perfect pup.

Golden Retriever

English Setter

Samoyed

Bernese
Mountain Dog

Labrador Retriever

Basset Hound

Pomeranian

Maltese

TIPS FOR ALL NEW PUPPY OWNERS
Aries through Pisces

First Days

The first day your pup spends with you and your family is full of excitement. This pup is adorable! You'll probably want to share him or her with all of your friends and neighbors. They may even drop over uninvited. Well, even if you are a Gemini, your first act of friendship with your pup is to discourage visitors for the first day or two.

To be adopted is a wonderful happening, but for your pup it's also tiring and very confusing. There are no familiar smells, Mom is gone, and even the rest of the litter have disappeared. Now that's scary. Lots of strangers about, even the nicest ones can make it even scarier, but that doesn't mean the pup is a wimp, Aries. It's just a baby.

It would be kinder to make your pup's trip home, and its entry into your family, as calm as possible. If you are driving the pup to your home, it would he helpful if another person is with you. Take along an old blanket or towel. This baby is not wearing a diaper. Paper towel in the car is a good idea, too, in case of travel upset. The pup may shiver or whimper, but that's nothing to worry about. If you are driving alone, the pup should be in a travel cage or box. Containing the pup will allow you to concentrate on your driving, knowing that the pup is safe, even if it is whimpering.

Introduce the pup to its bed as soon as the welcome party is over, and it has had the chance to relieve itself. Put something to cuddle into in its bed. An old blanket and safe soft toy is ideal, especially if the pup has just left its mother and litter. If someone has donated a soft toy with plastic eyes, remove them. The pup could choke on them.

If you don't have a dog bed, a cardboard box is fine so long as you remove or lower one side of it so that the pup can scramble in and out easily.

You'll probably have decided beforehand where to keep the pup for its own safety, and that of your home. If choosing to crate the pup, it would be a good idea to use the crate for the pup's first nap in your home. Baby gates are effective if you're confining the pup to a certain area. This is where its bed should be. Make sure that there are no loose, plugged in electrical cords about, and spread some newspaper on the floor for easier clean-ups.

In all probability, the pup will cry the first few nights in your home. It's just not used to the place yet. However, the adjustment will come more quickly if you keep a bedtime routine. Avoid scolding. It won't help, and will make the pup feel more miserable. Once you have checked that it has not got itself into trouble, say "Goodnight" in a firm and pleasant voice, and make your exit.

Accidents Happen

To housetrain your pup, first decide whether you want the dog to use the outdoors, or a newspaper in a corner, depending on where you live and your lifestyle. It's important to remember that the pup does not yet have control over its bladder or bowels. What do you do when the pup squats, and piddles on the floor? Well, pouncing on the pup, and smacking it, is not the way to go. The poor little thing won't have a clue as to why you've suddenly attacked it. Shoving the pup's nose in its puddle, and making threatening noises as you toss it outside, or onto its paper, is also old-fashioned, and ineffective. In fact, with some breeds, if you choose to use the old school methods, your dog could become a fear wetter, and you'll be having problems for the rest of its life. Fear wetting is known as "submissive urination", and is something you can avoid.

Understanding about this bladder and bowel control business, and teaching, not punishing, is the way to train your pup. When you catch your pup in the act, scoop it up and place it in the area you have chosen for such things. If the pup finishes there, praise it. Your pup will need to relieve itself about every two hours. A few minutes after the puppy has awakened from a nap, has eaten, or after a playful romp, carry the pup, or, preferably walk it, to where it should be squatting. It will go just in the right place by accident. Praise the pup - give it a treat. At first, the pup will not know why you're being extra nice, but it will learn the connection with repetition. If you don't clean up right away, the pup may get the idea of what's expected sooner. A previous deposit adds reinforcement, and pups often sniff an area before squatting. If you plan on paper training at first, and then want to transfer the pup's toilet facilities to the yard, it helps to place the pup's own soiled newspaper in the outside area preferred. Start by placing its paper by the door, and then just outside the door, until it makes the connection.

Some of you may be thinking of using a litter box with earth, sand or even kitty litter. That could be very messy. Dogs once hid their tracks by covering their waste matter, and the instinct is still there.

Chewing

Puppies chew a lot. They chew because they are losing their baby teeth, and gnawing on stuff really helps those itchy, sore gums. To avoid letting them find their own chewing material, such as your leather shoes, or a handy table leg, it's wise to invest in some chew toys from the pet store. Of course, your pup may still find your favorite shoes if you leave them out to be found. Chewed up shoes are not amusing. Some of you might even be tempted to use the damaged shoe to smack the pup, to teach it to stay away from your things. The problem with that approach is that it won't work, and could seriously hurt the puppy. A firm "no," to the shoe, followed by giving the pup its own chew toy will teach the lesson more effectively, particularly if you add "good dog" as it starts to chew on its own toy. Keep your chewable things away from the pup, or the pup away from your stuff, until it has its adult teeth.

Rawhide is a great chew. Most dogs love it. Rawhide satisfies the chewing need, and even helps to keep the dog's teeth clean. However, we have found that too much of this good thing can cause very loose stool. It's also wise to give rawhide when you are with the pup. It might try to swallow it whole, and choke on it.

Walks

It's unwise to take your pup out on the streets until it is protected from disease by its puppy shots. Check with your vet as to when the series of vaccinations are complete. Be sure to hold the pup on your lap on your first visits, or keep the pup in its carrier. Sick dogs have also seen their physician on those days.

Your pup's first collar should not fit too tightly. You must be able to slip a couple of fingers underneath it. Some of you may prefer to get a harness, but make sure you get the right size. You can get your puppy used to its leash right away, but go with the pup, and avoid pulling at this early stage. Walking on a leash is another thing your pup has to learn, and it will learn quickly and well if it's done positively. It's a good idea never to play tug-of-war with the leash, or allow the pup to chew on it. From the start, you should teach your pup that its leash is not a toy. If it decides otherwise, distract it by rattling paper or squeaking one of its toys, and put the leash away.

If you have a pup that will grow up to be a strong dog, you might consider starting the pup off with a gentle lead. Your dog would adjust to the restriction as a pup more easily than an adult dog.

Lost

Don't forget to have an ID on your dog's collar. We have returned several dogs to worried owners through their tags.

If you are concerned that your pup could be taken from your yard, or that your dog might run away, tracking a scent on the wind, you can have a chip implanted. This will enable you to find the pup. Your vet will be happy to discuss this option with you.

Food

Your pup's food and water bowls should be placed next to each other on some newspaper. Puppies are very messy eaters. Initially, your pup will need some nourishment four times a day. If you want to watch the pup eat, fine, but observe from a distance. This isn't the time to distract it. Check with the breeder as to what the pup is used to eating, and stick with this for the first few days until the pup has settled in your home. A change in diet can be made later if that's your choice. Your breeder or your vet will be pleased to discuss its nutritional needs with you. There should be fresh water in your pup's water bowl at all times. Be sure to change it daily. If you have a pup from one of the larger breeds, you will need to get a stand for its food bowl and water bowl when the dog has grown. Stooping too low to eat and drink could cause stomach upsets.

Obedience Training

Pick up a booklet to help you to train the breed of dog you have chosen. Doing it the right way will save lots of time, and avoid problems needing correction at a later date. Keep your training sessions short at first. A pup does not have a long attention span. It's not difficult to teach your pup your language if you remember to use simple commands, repeat them often, and avoid adding unnecessary words. Add the dog's name to your command, such as "Fenway, sit." Remember that small treats when the dog obeys you initially are good reward tools for learning listening skills. When the dog is doing something you prefer it not to do, try not to just yell the dog's name. You always need to use its name, and a command.

Your pup might be able to learn how to spell. When you spell out a magic word, such as "walk" to someone, hoping the keep the suggestion highly confidential, your pup will soon catch on.

If you think of your pup as a baby initially, and then as a toddler, needing guidance and affection from the start, the bonding process will begin immediately. A trusting relationship will form between you and your dog. In return for a few months of understanding and teaching, you'll have a dog you can depend upon to be your best friend for years. Of course, as in all relationships, it's good to start out with some compatibility, which is why AstroPups was written. Guarantees come with appliances, not pups, but we hope we have been of help to you.

Acknowledgements

We thank the authors listed below for supplying information to help us to make compatible matches, and recommend their books for informative reading.

All About Toy Dogs - Ricketts, Viva Leone
Book of All Terrier, The - Marvin, John T.
Companion Dogs - Liebers, Arthur
Dogs - Wratten, Peggy
Dogs of the World – Bongianni, Maurizio & Mori, Concetta
Life, History and Magic of the Dog - Mery, Ferdinand
Old English Sheepdog - Mandeville, John
Puppies - Spink, Kathryn
Shar-Pei - Nicholas, Anna Katherine
The Standard Guide to Pure-Bred Dogs - Glover, Harry
Ultimate Dog Book - Taylor, David

Made in the USA